Cambridge

Elements in Public Policy
edited by
M. Ramesh
National University of Singapore (NUS)
Michael Howlett
Simon Fraser University, British Colombia
Xun WU
Hong Kong University of Science and Technology
Judith Clifton
University of Cantabria
Eduardo Araral
National University of Singapore (NUS)

TRUTH AND POST-TRUTH IN PUBLIC POLICY: INTERPRETING THE ARGUMENTS

Frank Fischer

Humboldt University and University of Kassel, Germany

CAMBRIDGE
UNIVERSITY PRESS

CAMBRIDGE
UNIVERSITY PRESS

University Printing House, Cambridge CB2 8BS, United Kingdom

One Liberty Plaza, 20th Floor, New York, NY 10006, USA

477 Williamstown Road, Port Melbourne, VIC 3207, Australia

314–321, 3rd Floor, Plot 3, Splendor Forum, Jasola District Centre,
New Delhi – 110025, India

103 Penang Road, #05–06/07, Visioncrest Commercial, Singapore 238467

Cambridge University Press is part of the University of Cambridge.

It furthers the University's mission by disseminating knowledge in the pursuit of
education, learning, and research at the highest international levels of excellence.

www.cambridge.org
Information on this title: www.cambridge.org/9781108796071
DOI: 10.1017/9781108854344

© Frank Fischer 2021

First published 2021

A catalogue record for this publication is available from the British Library.

ISBN 978-1-108-79607-1 Paperback
ISSN 2398-4058 (online)
ISSN 2514-3565 (print)

In memory of Herbert Gottweis

Truth and Post-Truth in Public Policy: Interpreting the Arguments

Elements in Public Policy

DOI: 10.1017/9781108854344
First published online: November 2021

Frank Fischer
Humboldt University and University of Kassel, Germany

Author for correspondence: Frank Fischer, ffischer@gmx.com

Abstract: The phenomenon of post-truth poses a problem for the public policy-oriented sciences, including policy analysis. "Fake news" and the post-truth denial of facts constitute major concerns for numerous policy fields. Whereas a standard response is to call for more and better factual information, this Element shows that the effort to understand this phenomenon has to go beyond the emphasis on facts to include an understanding of the social meanings that get attached to facts in the political world of public policy. The challenge is thus seen to be as much about a politics of meaning as it is about epistemology. The approach here supplements the examination of facts with an interpretive policy-analytic approach to gain a fuller understanding of post-truth. The importance of the interpretive perspective lies in its ability to analyze policy knowledge in social context. This is illustrated through an examination of the policy arguments that have shaped the social and political controversies related to climate change and COVID-19 denial.

Keywords: truth, post-truth, policy sciences, knowledge, social meaning, values, arguments, climate denial, COVID-19 policy, interpretive policy analysis

ISBNs: 9781108796071 (PB), 9781108854344 (OC)
ISSNs: 2398-4058 (online), 2514-3565 (print)

Contents

Preface

This Element builds on and extends an inquiry about post-truth and climate denial introduced in an earlier essay (Fischer 2019).[1] The goals of this more elaborate study are twofold: the first is to examine the implications of post-truth and the spread of disinformation for public policy and policy analysis; the second is to show the way that interpretive policy analysis can help us better understand the politics associated with post-truth policy argumentation. After presenting the empirically oriented foundations of public policy studies, this contribution to the Element series examines specific political and epistemological issues pertinent to the post-truth challenge to policy analysis. Then, with the assistance of an interpretive logic of policy argumentation, the text assesses disinformation and fake news in the narrative-based arguments of those who deny climate change and COVID-19.

The general post-truth phenomenon and the specific cases are assessed from the perspective of interpretive social science and interpretive policy analysis in particular, with a focus on the social construction and interpretation of narratives and the arguments based on them. Whereas many critics of post-truth argue that the phenomenon can be traced to the relativism of postmodern constructivism, we argue here that this epistemic contention rests on a simplistic misunderstanding of constructivism and serves to divert attention away from the political motives that have given rise to post-truth as a tactic of denialism. Indeed, contrary to the critics, we seek to show that an interpretive policy-analytic approach is essential for an adequate understanding of post-truth politics. Interpretive policy analysis supplies an important postpositivist policy methodology – not to be confused with postmodernism – that can bring back the underlying politics of social meaning posed by post-truth.

It is not that facts are unimportant. Rather, it is that they gain meaning in the policy world from the social and political contexts to which they are applied. Thus, the social-subjective meanings that factual information have for political participants need to be brought into the analysis. Such social meanings are missing from standard empirically oriented policy methodologies, having long been methodologically ruled out of the analytical process. Here we show that social meanings, embedded in political narratives and articulated through policy arguments (also referred to as "narrative arguments"), are crucial explanatory factors. Indeed, it is the importance of such meanings that interpretive policy analysis seeks to draw out and emphasize.

The climate change example shows that better facts and fact-checking will not dissuade the deniers. They are more concerned with the political and social meanings attached to climate data than with the presentation of empirical

---

[1] The argument in the essay is restated here as part of this larger text, thanks to permission from Taylor and Francis.

evidence. They worry in particular about specific political interpretations of climate change and their meanings for the future of individual freedoms and a free-market society. In this regard, the politics of COVID-19 denial is remarkably similar, concerned as well with an ideological defense of personal freedoms and the fate of the economy. The analysis of the COVID-19 case turns more specifically to the processes of policy argumentation to examine the ways in which meanings drawn from ideological value orientations are used discursively to interpret factual data in denial arguments. The case shows how denial narratives and the arguments based on them are politically and methodologically constructed. Finally, this work offers some closing thoughts about how to deal with the major challenges this insidious post-truth phenomenon presents for both the policy-oriented sciences and, more broadly, democratic governance.

1 Introduction: Policy Science, Facts and the Post-Truth Challenge

One of the critical issues in political and policy discussions today is the role of post-truth in the form of "alternative facts" and fake news. It is a concern focused in particular on their meaning for democratic governance and its policymaking processes (McIntyre 2018; Davis 2017; Ball 2017; Kakutani 2018). Although there is nothing new about disinformation, fake facts and deception in politics, post-truth politics took on new importance after the British "Brexit" referendum to leave the European Union and the presidential election of Donald Trump, both in 2016. Before and after these political votes there has been an unprecedented barrage of false policy-oriented information disseminated through the media, especially social media, advancing claims with little or no basis in reality.

Formerly called "propaganda," this post-truth style of political communication, generally associated with the rise of populist politics, has a worrisome impact on both electoral and policy politics. Since its onslaught, this post-truth phenomenon has become an important – if not always new – political concern in other countries around the world, including Brazil, Hungary, the Philippines, Italy, Australia, Poland, Thailand and India, among others. In all of these countries, disinformation has come to influence and, in many cases, shape their policy deliberative processes. And there is no reason to believe that fake news will disappear after the electoral defeats of populist politicians (Mackintosh 2020; Baker 2020).

The pressing nature of this problem has led to a search for explanations. Given its complexity, a full treatment of this topic is beyond the scope of this

Element. In the United States, Britain and elsewhere, this would require in particular an examination of post-truth as the destructive outcome of the politics that has accompanied the rise of right-wing populism. As such, it is a consequence of a combination of intersecting political developments: a general "postdemocratic" decline in western democracies, right-wing strategies that fracture political cultures for sake of political gain, the subsequent rise of "tribal politics," the role of the social media and the politics of disinformation (Mann and Ornstein 2016: 31-80; Bennett and Livingston 2018). These developments have led to high levels of distrust, providing the underlying social basis of post-truth (D'Ancona 2017; Lewis 2016; Kahan 2017).

1.1 Knowledge for Policy

This analysis narrows the topic to an exploration of the meaning and implications of post-truth as it impacts the role of knowledge and facts in public policy. By and large, the main attempts to understand and deal with post-truth have focused on the importance of defending factual knowledge, if not truth per se, with a dominant emphasis on better facts and fact-checking strategies (Kavanagh and Rich 2020). This focus is understandable, but it runs into explanatory limitations. As argued here, such an understanding of post-truth largely rests on an empirical and overly objective understanding of policy knowledge. Whereas most people take the meaning of empirical objectivity to be relatively clear, work in the sociology and philosophy of science shows this concept to be more complicated epistemologically than would otherwise appear to be obvious.

Many writers have sought to place the blame for the post-truth phenomenon on the rise of postmodernist relativism and the interpretive methods of social constructivism (Andersen 2017). These are portrayed as having irresponsibly laid the groundwork for the post-truth rejection of established facts. But this is a limited view, as we argue herein. Moreover, we seek to show that the interpretive-analytic approach of a constructivist perspective, rather than being the culprit, is an epistemological orientation that can help us sort out and better understand post-truth arguments.

1.2 Post-Truth and Policy Science

Post-truth, not surprisingly, has created considerable concern on the part of both government officials and expert policy communities. It has led governments around the world to establish policies and programs – commissions, committees, watchdog groups and the like – to deal with the problem of disinformation (Farkas and Schou 2020: 87–95). In addition, it has given rise to a great deal of concern in the social and political sciences, including the applied policy-oriented disciplines.

Not only does post-truth pose a challenge to commonly held understandings about democracy – especially the belief that it depends on a commitment to truthful knowledge from multiple perspectives – it also raises fundamental questions about the core mission of the social sciences. Specifically, it challenges science's basic commitment to a truth-oriented pursuit of facts, as elusive as that might prove to be. Indeed, the concept of post-truth portends a fundamental challenge to the very raison d'etre of rigorous social and political inquiry. For a policy science, moreover, the issue is especially crucial, as it is more on the front lines of politics that other forms of academic social science.

The policy science orientation, as such, is designed to supply reliable information and advice to real-world policy decision-makers (Lasswell and Lerner 1951; Dunn 2019). Since the 1960s, when it became more common to speak of "policy analysis," the discipline has increasingly been shaped by a positivist understanding of knowledge, in particular as it is manifested in the methods of modern economics, the empiricist social science par excellence (Robert and Zechhauser 2010). Economic analysis, in fact, supplies the dominant methodologies for current policy-analytic practices.

Given this empirical search for the facts, the rise of post-truth, also referred to as "post-factualism," has led many contemporary scholars in the social and policy sciences to fret – not surprisingly – about the import of the challenge to the empirical methods and practices of the disciplines (Fischer 2019; Perl, Howlett and Ramesh 2018). This has especially been the case in countries where right-wing politicians have come to power, most notably in the United States and the United Kingdom. Suddenly, post-truthers were in charge of the agencies the policy sciences are designed to serve. What is more, political leaders such as Trump set out to eliminate expert reports, restrict data collection, remove expert advisory commissions, shift decision-making away from expert regulatory commissions and the like (Nichols 2019).

Despite the widespread expression of worries about the implications of post-truth among policy experts, however, there is not a lot of literature on post-truth and policy science per se. The literature that does exist generally holds to a relatively standard policy-analytic argument for better factual evidence. A case in point is an essay on policymaking models and "truthiness" by Perl, Howlett and Ramesh (2018). After exploring the epistemological challenges posed by various types of disinformation and ignorance, the authors examine the most prominent policy models – including the policy cycle heuristic, the advocacy coalition framework and the multiple streams model – to determine what sorts of difficulties they confront in reconciling "the new reality of false or evidence free policy making" (p. 583). These approaches, they conclude, can resiliently handle policy deliberations and decision-making processes that have to deal with disinformation and distorted factual claims. As they put it, "the 'standard' policy sciences frameworks themselves are quite robust and capable ... of identifying the key features of the new policy process" which have emerged in the wake of the emergence of truthiness and also the challenges policymakers face in creating and controlling policy problems and processes "in a world filled with post-factual inputs and influences" (Perl et al. 2018: 583). They find, in short, better facts to be the solution to post-factuality. Further, they aver that the underlying problem can be traced to what they identify as a kind of "post-positivist anomie," whereby political discourse, normative beliefs and social identity are mixed in with, and at times indistinguishable from, factual policy evidence.

1.3 Interpretive Social Science and Public Policy

There can be no argument against the contention that better information is important for effective policymaking. But what if the ground beneath these empirical models has shifted? What if we have, in fact, moved into something of a postpositivist world in which there is no turning back? What if the understanding of what constitutes a fact is the very thing in question and needs a new, nonpositivist understanding? And what if instrumental rationality turns out to provide only one kind of knowledge relevant to the policy process? These are the sorts of questions that postpositivist policy scholars put forward. They offer, moreover, a different epistemological model for policy studies that deals directly with this challenge. Indeed, as we shall see, a postpositivist interpretive approach to knowledge offers a useful way to understand the post-truth phenomenon.

Although this perspective is generally identified by the critics of post-truth politics as "postmodern" (MacItyre 2018: 123–150), the methods of interpretive social science, and interpretive policy analysis (Yanow 2000; Münch 2016) in particular, are not necessarily postmodern. It is a mistake to confuse them for one and the same thing, especially if it means rejecting the interpretive perspective. To do so, we argue, limits the effort to adequately understand the phenomenon. We seek, in just this regard, to show that an interpretive policy-analytic perspective can in fact offer a better way of conceptualizing the post-truth controversy. It can do this by bringing back an analysis of the essential subjective dimensions inherent to post-truth politics.

Before presenting the interpretive policy-analytic perspective, however, it is important to gain a better grasp of post-truth and the political and discursive struggles that it has ushered in. Toward this end, we look more closely in the next section at the definitions of post-truth, fake news and the politics behind the denial of facts.

2 Post-Truth Defined

The concept of post-truth, as it concerns us here, emerged in 2015 during the campaigns for the Brexit referendum and the election of Donald Trump. It had such a rapid rise that Oxford Dictionaries labeled it the "word of the year" in 2016, after a 2,000 percent increase in usage (Flood 2016). Although the term has no fixed meaning, the idea that we have moved into a post-truth world became a major topic of discussion and debate. According to the dictionary, "post-truth" is defined as "relating to or denoting circumstances in which objective facts are less influential in shaping public opinion than appeals to emotions." It refers to "a political culture in which debate is framed largely by appeals to emotion disconnected from the details of policy, and by the repeated assertion of talking points to which factual rebuttals are ignored." As such, post-truth "differs from traditional contesting and falsifying of facts by relegating facts and expert opinions to be of secondary importance relative to appeal to emotion" (Flood 2016). The dictionary further describes it as a word that captures the "ethos, mood or preoccupations of that particular year," and as having "lasting potential as a word of cultural significance."

For the duration of a grueling political campaign leading up to the US presidential election in 2016, blatant post-truth lies and so-called "alternative facts" circulated freely in political speeches and media reporting. So problematic was this that it has led to nothing less than a fact-checking industry. While factual worries could be uncovered everywhere, such investigations found that Donald Trump's relationship to truth has been deeply problematic.[2]

2.1 Post-Truth and Fake News

It is also important to discuss the relationship of post-truth to "fake news," as the two concepts often accompany one another. Although closely related, they are not the same. The essential foundation of post-truth is established, following McDermott (2019: 218), as being "when people consider opinion to be as legitimate as confirmed facts, or when emotional factors weigh as heavily as statistical evidence. When these tendencies hold sway among even a significant minority of the public, they can exert a strong influence on public-policy

---

[2] Trump's flagrant neglect of the "facts" has been described as socio-pathological (Croucher 2019).

debates as well as on behavioral outcomes," voting being an important case in point. This leads to what can be called "post-truth culture."

Fake news, on the other hand, can be differentiated from post-truth because it mainly involves the spread of false statements.[3] To be understood as fake news, a story must be put forward with the deliberate intent to mislead or deceive the recipient – the reader or listener – for the purposes of political objectives or financial gain. It can be described as an "empty signifier," which in itself carries no meaning but can be attached to anything (Farkus and Schou 2019). Despite its difference to post-truth, however, some argue that the increase in fake news, accelerated by social media, laid the groundwork for post-truth.

2.2 Spread of Post-Truth, Fake News and "Truthiness"

Today, examples of post-truth and fake news falsehoods are so extensive that they are beyond counting. They range from the more traditional variety, such as denial of the Holocaust, to more contemporary examples of falsehoods designed to influence the outcome of political elections, the machinations of foreign political leaders, the refusal to accept the effectiveness of vaccinations, the denial of climate change, myths about the origins of the COVID-19 and election denials. There is scarcely an issue that has not been affected.

Trump, it has been shown, holds the record when it comes to the spread of fake news, sheer lies and falsehoods. (Kessler, Rizzo and Kelly 2020). And, more than a little curiously, this has had only a small effect on his relationship with Republican voters, and next to none on his so-called support base. Even more perversely, they have held him to be more honest than Hillary Clinton. Underlying this are the populist movements in the United States and abroad that continue to be fueled by the rise of social media, the primary mechanism for spreading fake news and disinformation. In terms of populist politics, post-truth social media can be understood as a response to a growing distrust of the political establishment and the media – both their ideas and their practices.

It is certainly not the case that the spread of lies is unknown to politics; indeed, it is as old as the profession itself (Arendt 1972). To take just one prominent political example, George Orwell described political propaganda during the Spanish Civil War as fundamental to the struggle. In Orwellian style, he argued that "the very concept of objective truth" seemed to be "fading out of the world" (Orwell and Angus 1980: 295–296). He worried about how history would record the Spanish war if Franco won and his propagandists were to become the historians. Given that the government relied on the spread of

---

[3] For a history of fake news, see Czarniawska (2021).

disinformation and lies, he wondered if people would forget what had actually happened, especially after those who could remember the war had died? Would the propaganda be believed, he worried? Would it become universally accepted, with lies turning into the truth?

So problematic is the situation today that various writers have expressed the same concern – namely, whether or not history could be truthfully written in the future. Very problematically, political systems are now so divided that there is "a battle between two ways of perceiving the world, two fundamentally different approaches to reality," between which one has to decide (D'Ancona 2017: 5). It is a point that can easily be tested. One need only compare the political reporting of Fox News with that of MNSBC on American television. Their interpretations of the same events often leave the impression that they are coming from different planets. Their respective coverage of the Trump impeachment hearing brought this phenomenon to new heights, only later to be surpassed by false claims about election fraud and COVID-19.

2.3 Truthiness

Arguably, Trump's lying has been qualitatively different from the sort of falsehoods that politicians have spread up to this point. Indeed, the contemporary use of the concept of truth in various ways no longer directly relates to truthfulness. In the words of the comedian Stephen Colbert, it can better be described as a kind of "truthiness," referring to the phenomenon of believing a statement to *feel* true, even though it is not supported by factual evidence (Watson 2016). In view of the attention that has been given to this interpretation of post-truth, Merriam-Webster included "truthiness" in its dictionary, stating that it cleared a way for a post-truth world "in which the feel of truth, or "truthiness" is the only thing that matters" (Zimmer 2010).

3 Post-Truth: Ignorance and "Anything Goes"

The emergence of post-truth is, certainly on the surface, a major threat to science and social as well as physical inquiry. Insofar as rigorously pursuing truthful facts with tested methods is the raison d'etre of science, post-truth challenges its very core. It is seen as leading to a form of irrationalism that offers no firm basis for developing the solid, policy-oriented facts required for the guidance of society. Indeed, this poses a fundamental worry for most contemporary institutions, techno-bureaucratic in nature, that are designed to assemble and apply confirmed facts to the policy issues confronting modern society. Indeed, the strategy of "evidence-based" policymaking has emerged in recent times to assist these organizations with the tasks at hand (Young et al. 2002).

More than a few have worried that postmodern thought and its focus on the relativity of truth has played a major role in bringing about post-truth and the idea of alternative facts. So worried is the scientific community about the rejection of facts that it organized a large "March for Science" protest in Washington, DC (Vence and Grant 2017). The predominant counter-response, especially by the media, has been to emphasize "fact-checking." This is an approach that has been of particular concern in dealing with the pressing problem of climate change, but later the focus turned to COVID-19 as well.

3.1 Agnotology

On a more sophisticated level, this worry has led various scholars to move beyond the emphasis on established facts and acknowledge the failure to understand the role of ignorance, in particular the ways ignorance is shaped and constructed. Indeed, this concern about disinformation has led to a new field of ignorance studies called "agnotology." As Proctor and Schiebinger (2008) point out, scholars have focused on the production of scientifically tested knowledge at the expense of ignorance, which can also be systematically produced to serve particular purposes. There is a large literature on how to avoid ignorance, but little on ignorance itself, despite its pervasiveness. For Proctor and Schiebinger, the distribution and maintenance of ignorance is a much-neglected element in the current post-factual world. A point central to the post-truth debate, they stress a need to also study the reasons and purposes for the maintenance of ignorance, particularly as it pertains to post-truth.

3.2 Ignorance and Relativism: Science Wars Redux

Those who take postmodernism to be promoting a form of ignorance launch their primary response at its critique of science. Scholars of postmodern persuasion, along with many in the fields of cultural studies and science studies, have been lambasted for raising questions about the nature and practices of science. In various ways, the struggle is more than a little reminiscent of the earlier "science wars" debates of the 1990s between cultural theorists and members of the scientific community (Ross 1996; Berube 2011). These exchanges, often caustic in nature, focused on the claim that science is founded on social, political and cultural factors. Basic to this culturally oriented "deconstruction" of what science does and how it works has been a rejection of the idea that stable definitions of reality can exist, thus undercutting the possibility of universal truths. Although the target of these debates has typically been the physical and natural sciences, it also extends to economics and the social sciences more generally (Graber 2019).

Over time, this critique of science has given rise to a postpositivist understanding of science that emphasizes the relative, uncertain, contextually site-specific and language-based character of knowledge. The debate, which has vacillated between epistemological sophistication and ad hominem argument, turns on questions about the nature of reality. Is knowledge about reality something "out there" to be uncovered independently of human ideas, as the scientific community generally contends, or is all knowledge, to one degree or another, socially constructed and thus dependent on human conventions? In this postpositivist view, all disciplines need to critically rethink their basic principles in light of these social influences, a view rigorously resisted and rejected by most members of the scientific community, preferring instead to hold onto their foundational myth of "the search for objective truth."

For the opponents of postmodernism, cultural studies and social constructivism, these modes of inquiry are seen to lead to the view that all facts are just matters of opinion. By denying the possibility of truths that are eternal or ideal, the approach is accused of allowing for "anything goes" (Sokal 2008). Such relativism is thus seen to enable an ignorant world in which all competing positions are believed to make equally valid truth claims. However, in the view of theorists who've grappled with relativism, it is not necessarily the case that there are no standards for judging what is good or what is right. Rather, it means recognizing that such standards are the products of conventions and assessments that are always context dependent (Stanford Encyclopedia of Philosophy 2020).

These ongoing criticisms have led a seminal figure in cultural studies – none less than Bruno Latour (2018) – to assert that the time has come for postmodernists to now reestablish "some of the authority of science." Worrying in particular about the denial of climate change, without altogether rejecting the social elements in scientific conduct, he calls for a revision of the more problematic relationship to reality put forth by the radical critics of science. But this does not mean a rejection of interpretivism, which, as we shall see, need not mean anything goes.

Much of the discussion, however, overlooks the possibility that post-truth may reflect a deeper – even insidious – phenomenon that is about more than established scientific facts per se. While fact-checking is a worthy activity, we need to look deeper into this development to find out what it is about, what is behind it. Toward this end, we look next at "post-truth culture."

4 The Political Rise of the Post-Truth Culture

Post-truth is first and foremost the outcome of the destructive politics that has invaded modern political systems, especially in the United States and Britain.

While a full discussion of the political factors behind the rise of post-truth and alternative facts is beyond the scope of this Element, it is important to point to the basic political dynamics behind its emergence. Even this is not easy as the post-truth phenomena is the consequence of a combination of intersecting political developments: for example, the general decline of democratic politics, a right-wing strategy to fracture the political culture for conservative political gain, the subsequent rise of tribal politics, the role of social media and the politics of disinformation (Bennet and Livingston 2021).

It is first a story of general democratic decline – what some writers have discussed in terms of a new era of "post-democracy" and the manipulation of information that is part of that theory. But more specifically in the United States, it is in many ways the consequence of a political strategy on the part of the conservatives to fracture the political culture. More often than not, political parties now treat each other with animosity, and political commentators have begun to speak of political "tribes" rather than parties. In this game, the goal is to protect one's own tribe regardless of the issue or concern at hand. And it's within this context that the idea of "alternative facts" has emerged. When one of the tribes does not like the outcome of a particular policy study, they dismiss it as "their facts, not ours!"

The influence of such disinformation is difficult to measure, but there is plenty of evidence to make it a troubling reality (Farkus and Schou 2019). As such, it has become the subject of various investigatory bodies, ranging from the US House and Senate to the CIA and FBI. Much of the investigation conducted by these bodies has been concerned with the role of Russian hacking, which has been used strategically to turn the internet into a political weapon. But it has also focused on social media well, in particular Facebook and Twitter (Farkus and Schou 2019). It is a concern that has spread to other countries as well, such as Germany, France and the United Kingdom.

4.1 Political Tribes and the Politics of "Just Say No"

Such feelings about the opposing party are so strongly negative that anything a group says is questioned and rejected just because "the other side" is saying it, giving rise to a strategy of "just say no." This emotionally based "behavioral polarization" – characterized by anger toward the other side, active commitment to one's own party and a tendency to view positions through a biased political lens – is motivated more by a sense of team spirit than by the substance of policy issues. Such tribes, particularly populist tribes, are based on anti-establishment ideologies and often described with terms such as secular religion, like-minded brethren, catechism of sacred beliefs, demonology, political cult and righteous devotion to their causes (Farkus and Schou 2019; Packer 2018). Tribal identification becomes the basis of a team that has to be defended at all costs against the evil other. Large numbers of conservatives, for example, support climate denial simply because it is part of membership in their tribe (Nyhan 2021).

While politics is typically presented as being about the competition of interests and ideas, tribal politics puts the emphasis on power and the need to make sure that scarce resources are allocated to "our" people, whatever it takes (Lewis 2016). It is in this "weaponized" context of tribalism that fake news emerges as an important resource in the political struggle, whereby political survival assumes greater importance than facts. In the course of the struggle, the ends come to be seen as justifying the means; disinformation emerges as a justifiable political strategy.

4.2 Cultural Cognition and Motivated Reason

From an analytical perspective, Kahan's (2017) "Cultural Cognition Project" helps to explain the intellectual dynamics of this clash of political beliefs. In the case of climate change, for example, Kahan attributes the close correlation between "worldview" and acceptance or rejection of climate change research to a process of "cultural cognition." This points to the way in which people process new data or information in terms of their relationship to their preferred political orientation and the "vision of the good society" it supports. As Kahan (2010: 296) explains, people have trouble believing that courses of action or behaviors that they find admirable are in fact damaging to society and, conversely, that actions that they believe to be "bad" are actually beneficial to society. Insofar as accommodating such a disturbing view can "drive a wedge between them and their peers, they have a strong emotional predisposition to reject it." In short, they find it easier to reject reality claims than to observe damage or destruction to their political worldview. History, in fact, abounds with such examples of "motivated reason."

If powerful belief systems are forced to confront problematic evidence, they seldom fade and disappear altogether (Kolberg 2017). Instead, they can develop cult status, even if marginalized. In the process, the believers come see the problem not as intrinsic to their belief or worldview, but rather a result of failures by biased political or scientific leaders to exercise the appropriate intellectual or scientific rigor. Instead of reconsidering their beliefs, as in the case of climate research, they prefer to shoot the messenger.

4.3 Fact Resistance: The Need *Not* to Know

In the case of post-truth, this has led to a perverse situation in which certain segments of these societies – the so-called "base" in Trump's America – have hardened their ideas and beliefs to such a degree that they can be described as "fact resistant." Indeed, as Gitlin (2020:50) puts it, they "[live] in falsehood." Many of them know that the views they hold conflict with demonstrated facts, but they've learned to live with this cognitive disconnect. Research shows that a fair number of them understand that they support ideas that they do not themselves entirely believe in; that is, they do not wholly believe their own convictions. Some of them seem to rationalize discordant information, while others seek to spin or evade factual information that counters their beliefs. As Gitlin (2020:50) explains it, they have "a need not to know." Research on "cognitive dissonance," focused on such mental stress, demonstrates that when confronted with a conflict between evidence and beliefs, believers will tend to hang on to their beliefs if they are practically and emotionally invested in them.

Some admit that they willingly retain these false views, often based on lies, because they believe it will lead to a greater good. That is, many of them know that Trump tells lies, but accept this because he is seen to represent their last line of defense against what they view as a repugnant political system they've identified with the Democratic Party. Gitlin argues that it is not unlikely that Trump's base's commitment to him "can outlast many disappointments insofar as they can be blamed on the treachery of his unrelenting enemies" (Gitlin 2020: 59). It is a point dramatically reflected in their unwillingness to accept his loss of the 2020 presidential election. It is a reality that is not limited to those with low levels of education: it includes many conservatives with a college degree.

5 Emotion and Post-Truth: Living with Falsehoods

How do people convince themselves to believe in and act upon things that are not true? An important part of the answer relates to emotional commitments. Although this is a complicated topic that cannot be discussed here in detail, it is important to recognize that emotion is an essential component in helping people to paste over contradictory beliefs and falsehoods. Indeed, emotion is part of the definition of post-truth and thus discussion of its role is required, even if brief.

As we have already suggested, post-truth arguments can be understood as a fusing of emotion with information. Indeed, this can arguably be the definition of "truthiness," understood as an argument or claim conditioned by a particular emotional orientation. It refers to the accepting of a claim as true because it *feels* true, even though it is not supported by verified information or know-ledge – that is, something that has the "feel of truth." Appeals to emotion – disconnected from factual details – are thus becoming more important in the forming of public opinion than is demonstrable evidence. Emotional appeals, as noted, are often now juxtaposed to evidence-based policymaking.

There has been a long-standing lack of attention to the role of emotions in the social sciences, and in the field of public policy in particular, which has only begun to be corrected in more recent years. Although those in the practical world of politics have always recognized the emotional nature of political controversies, the social sciences traditionally sought to rule out emotion as "irrational" and thus not amenable to rigorous analysis. Indeed, much of the early history of the social sciences was devoted to substituting emotionally laden value issues with objectively verified knowledge. Today, the renewed attention in an era of post-truth can only be a welcome development, as an understanding of the role of emotion and passion is of critical importance for grasping post-truth politics (Durnova 2019).

To come to grips with the post-truth phenomena, we need to recognize that earlier understandings of the role of emotion are antiquated. We have subsequently learned, with significant help from neuroscience, that emotions are not necessarily irrational and problematic (Markus 2002). Rather, they can be meaningful responses – a form of "emotional sense-making" – that help people take notice of things, such as events, ideas, understandings and perceptions, that they consider important and usually in need of relatively immediate attention. Emotions can, for example, alert and prepare people for the appearance of dangerous enemies – "Mexican rapists" crossing the border – or they can help rally appreciation and affection for a particular political leader – as witnessed by the passionate demonstrations on the part of Trump's political base. If these people come to believe that the "deep state" is about to engineer a political overthrow of their duly elected leaders, they will appeal to Trump to save them.

5.1 Narrative Emotions as Mix of Feeling and Belief

Emotions can be analyzed in a number of ways. Particularly relevant for an understanding post-truth is an analysis of the role of emotions in stories, or "narrative emotions" (Keen 2015: 152–161). For example, from this perspective we can explore the ways that the political rhetoric of populist narratives is tied to particular emotional responses (Durnova 2019; Kleres 2010). Here, the theorizing of Nussbaum (2001) is helpful. She has illustrated how emotional influence works to shape the "inner landscape" of our political lives, both mentally and socially. Such inner emotional landscapes – right-wing populist or liberal progressive, for example – operate as deep dispositions toward political situations, particularly as they relate to group interests and values. If events point to political actions judged to be beneficial – "clean the swamp" –

the inner landscape generates positive feelings, and, conversely, worrisome feelings if the situation or event poses problems or dangers – for example, Hillary Clinton's pedophiles preying on young children.

There are, in this regard, good emotions that play constructive roles (compassion and love) and bad emotions (hate and anger) that lead to destructive consequences. In positive terms, Nussbaum (2001) points to the essential role of beneficial emotions for social solidarity, identify and harmony. This need for solidarity and group identity is often associated with basic emotions expressed by alienated people who feel that society has left them behind. Unfortunately, this need to assuage such feelings can render them susceptible to populist disinformation that plays to their biases in reassuring ways. Indeed, Trump regularly sought to exploit these emotional needs for political gain. This susceptibility, moreover, is perhaps even more likely for people locked down because of COVID-19. With little outside contact, many can only make supportive contacts with other anxious citizens online via social media.

5.2 Emotion and Intelligence

Further, emotions are themselves suffused with tacit knowledge. In Nussbaum's view, emotions are a composite mix of feelings and beliefs. They can thus serve as deeper sources of awareness, social understanding and critical judgment. Emotions can trigger thoughts and beliefs, but the latter can also be the initiators of emotions, and emotional responses are forms of intelligent reactions that can in important ways be dealt with through persuasion. This is a point demonstrated time and again in the disagreements over governmental measures to deal with COVID-19. For those who think that a societal lockdown is a secret strategy for elites to gain greater political control, the story itself can generate emotional outrage, which can lead to public protest in the streets, and even to taking guns to the state capitol. People are typically emotionally excited by things they consider to be unjust or wrong. The beliefs they hold may be "erroneous and their anger unreasonable but their behavior is intelligent and cognitive in the sense that it is grounded upon a belief which may be criticized and even altered by argumentation" (Fortenbaugh 1975: 17). But this possibility depends to a significant degree on a level of trust and commitment on the part of those manning the post-truth barricades. And trust is just what is missing.

Post-truth and the tribal politics to which it has given rise have, in short, dramatically thrown up emotional barriers that block the possibility of meaningful discourse. Fundamental to these impediments in modern social and political processes is the media, particularly social media. Through the mass media, especially television and the internet, emotions play a large role in the communication of information. With the emergence of a commercially oriented entertainment format, even news reporting becomes something akin to an emotional construction of social reality. Truth, in this context, is often judged by the degree to which it *feels* genuine (Fischer 2019; MacIntyre 2018: 63–122). It is now a phenomenon closely related to the rise of post-truth culture.

6 Social Media and Disinformation

It would be difficult to underestimate the role of right-wing social media outlets in the distribution of false news. Writers such as Bennet and Livingston (2018: 122) describe such disinformation as "intentional falsehoods spread as news stories or simulated documentary formats to advance political goals." It involves "systematic disruptions of authoritative information flows due to strategic deceptions that may appear very credible to those who consume them."[4] While there are some radical left networks also distributing disinformation, the tendency is more common on the radical right. It emerges as part of a more general attack on the press, described by Trump as "the enemy of the people."

Attacking the press, to be sure, is not new. But Bennett and Livingston find a distinction between attacking the press and the contemporary politics of disinformation. Essentially, the latter is a strategy conceived to divide the information system itself, the result of which is now an underlying division between the mainstream media and those of the alternative conservative movement. People counted among the radical right in the United States, as well as in other lands, can now find competing social media advancing alternative versions of social and political reality.

In earlier eras there were comparatively fewer media channels through which official information passed. During those times, trust in institutions and the information they purveyed was much higher than today. As Bennett and Livingston explain (2018: 128), "the combination of higher trust and fewer public information sources enabled both authorities and the press to exercise more effective gatekeeping against wild or dangerous narratives from the social fringes or foreign adversaries." But the contemporary mix of volatile hate, disinformation, media outlets and institutional corrosion has facilitated oppositional groups in transitioning into destructive, undemocratic political forces in many countries, as the alternative social media has reached larger and larger followers, and served to assist populist movements in achieving significantly

---

[4] Disinformation differs from misinformation. Whereas misinformation is simply false regardless of intent, disinformation involves an deliberate intention to mislead or deceive.

higher level of electoral gains. Often facilitated by right-wing think tanks (Landry 2020), the essential goal of the mobilization of radical right groups has been the creation of "information silos" that seek to exclude and denigrate those who offer different views. These include, among other things, the spread of cultural stories that challenge the essential commitments to democratic freedoms, political tolerance and the norms of evidence and reason intrinsic to informed civic discussion.

The breakdown of authority in political institutions, together with an increase in alternative information channels (generating political myths for consumption by political tribe members), leads many people to seek out and support parties and movements removed from the mainstream, particularly on the right (Bennett and Livingston 2021). As these radical right movements reject the core institutions of the press and politics, often hostilely so, a political environment emerges that is conducive to the spread of mythologies, such as myths about climate change and COVID-19. Both the political left and the right have sought to bend the social media to serve their own purposes, but such efforts have been of far greater significance on the right than on the left. The emergence of what has been called the "media echo chamber" has its roots in the rise of conservative talk radio in the latter part of the 1980s, later to be dramatically ramped up by an astonishing array of social media platforms, including Twitter, radical websites, YouTube, Facebook, WikiLeaks and Astroturf think tanks, operated by an array of communications professionals, among others (Jamieson and Capella 2010; Farkas and Schou 2020).

6.1 Alternative Social Media as Post-Truth Response to Political-Cultural Upheaval

The post-truth phenomenon is, in short, better understood in terms of political struggles than in terms of intellectual debates about knowledge and epistemics, which is not to suggest that the latter are unimportant. Post-truth, as we discuss it today, has emerged from a convergence of nefarious events that is generally dated from 2016, but arguably with roots in the political deceptions that trace back to Bush's and Blair's fabricated justifications for the Iraq wars, if not earlier. In any case, the contemporary problem is anchored in a growing anxiety that has emerged around the world over the past decade, thanks in significant part to the destructive outcomes of neoliberal global markets, the hardships resulting from the financial meltdown of 2008, the emergence of migration jeopardizing some peoples' economic and social security, and the troublesome realities of climate change, to mention only the most obvious sources of angst (Latour 2018; McIntyre 2018).

While these existential worries had somewhat different origins in different places around the globe, the common anxieties result from the general feeling that things are not under control and are experienced as increasing levels of economic risk and social uncertainty. Many people have, in fact, seen their standard of living fall significantly, while others feel threatened by growing the migration they believe to be responsible for their social and economic precariousness. To this we need to add perceived levels of crime and violence, high costs of living, unaffordable health care, the decline in upward mobility, stagnant wages, automation and the deterioration of traditional family structures, among other factors. This has led to precarious degrees of distrust of the political elites and institutions taken to be responsible for the current turmoil, frequently portrayed as a crisis of liberal representative governance (Tomey 2016). As liberal political elites and the mainstream media have largely failed to adequately represent or portray the interests and concerns of the lower-middle and working classes, a political void has opened, which right-wing media could step into and exploit with alternative facts and narratives (Bennett and Livingston 2021). Here, no falsehood circulated by the right-wing social media has played a greater role than the idea that migrants are stealing jobs, are exploiting social welfare systems and are engaged in violent criminal acts, including raping white women.

6.2 Social Media and the Paranoid Style of Politics

This anxiety-driven search for new political narratives to explain these worrisome realities has led to widespread dissatisfaction with the politics and policies of the established political parties. Indeed, it has given rise to new political cleavages, often extreme enough to be referred to as "political tribes," especially in the United States and the United Kingdom. Driven by growing feelings of alienation, these tribes bring together people who share suspicions, and even emotional hostilities, toward both the ruling elites and the opposing tribes. It is not unusual, given the levels of estrangement, for conspiracy theories to emerge, as Richard Hofstadter showed decades ago in his book on the "paranoia style" of politics. In the case of climate change and COVID-19 in the United States, for example, it is framed as a deep state conspiracy aimed to impose a left-wing political agenda.

Despite the long history of paranoia-style conspiracies, Rosenblum and Muirhead (2019) find a difference between present-day conspiracy theories and those of yesterday. As conspiracies have shifted from the margins of society to mainstream politics, including the corridors of power, the demand for evidence and explanation has fallen away. Whereas it was normal in earlier periods to seek out evidence in support of claims, the demand for explanation has gone. Now, the purveyors of conspiracies simply impose their own reality and reinforce it with constant repetition rather than evidence. As they put it, conspiracists simply circulate their claims under the cover of lots of "people are saying . . ."

Explaining why people are susceptible to conspiracy theories is challenging. A considerable amount of social and psychological research has attempted to answer this question (Moyer 2019). Whereas the deniers constitute no monolithic group with just one point of view (Bokat-Lindell 2021), a number of psychological features can be identified that help to explain the phenomenon. They include people who feel superior to their fellow citizens (especially those who feel down and out) and look for reasons to justify their superior status. Some believe they have access to information less known, even secret, that others – dumb or blind – do not possess, and feel obligated to make it known. There are also disadvantaged groups, especially the economically downtrodden and socially depressed, for whom it is important to have villains to blame for their situation. Conspiracy theories offer them an outlet to explain away their own hard luck and lack of social standing.

What has made this struggle with disinformation particularly pernicious is the rise of the new internet-based social media. If various elements of this post-truth bricolage could have been found in other times, what is distinctive now is the presence of social media and its ability to greatly speed up the circulation of political messages (typically anonymously unattached to their senders). This has been an essential – some would say *the* essential – feature of post-truth politics today. The new media – found on Facebook, Google, Twitter, Instagram and YouTube internet platforms – send messages that can quickly go viral, circulating and recirculating at unprecedented speeds. Facilitated by the use of sophisticated algorithms and bots that collect and distribute information, the messages are fed to people – on both the political right and the left – in ways that either substantiate their established biases or create new ones. In the case of the radical right, they serve both unintentionally and intentionally to attract unknowing, but susceptible media consumers to right-wing websites that spew out hate messages that target Muslims, blacks, Jews, liberal politicians and others with inflammatory rhetoric. (Research shows that while young people are often the target of these efforts, people over 65 seem to be the most susceptible). The pervasiveness and repetition of the messages give them a sense of credibility – or, at least, they seed enough doubt in their followers to keep them tuned in. Indeed, the messages are intentionally designed to traffic in both "alternative facts" and outright falsehoods.

6.3 The Disinformation Industry

Beyond the vitriolic politics of the various tribes, deceptions and lies have been dramatically exacerbated by the emergence of a false formation industry that has found insidious ways to strategically invade and manipulate social media (Bennett and Livingston 2018; Edelman 1988). Right-wing sites, including online publications such as Breitbart News, do this to supply particular political tribes with strategic messages, but many of them also move beyond political messaging to promote deeper conspiratorial segments of these societies, such as Neo-Nazis, anti-government militias, fundamentalist religious groups and organized foreign interests dedicated to sowing turmoil in domestic politics (as illustrated by the Russian invasion of social media to influence the US elections in 2016). Using fake media accounts, these hackers invent messages hostile to particular political candidates that can be relayed and echoed thousands of times throughout the information ecosystem.

These things start in dark corners of the web, where conspiracy theories are created and pushed. "Outlandish theories burble up from the depths and are laundered through increasingly mainstream channels," such as Fox News, before they reach politicians like ex-president Trump (Warzel 2020). After being amplified by top-level politicians, these fake theories are given more credence as they are echoed in the right-wing media, which then leads a Trump to amplify them even further. One of the most astonishing cases involved the claim that a "deep state" liberal overthrow of the Trump Administration would lead to civil war in the United States (Warzel 2019). It started on right-wing media, but went viral when Trump retweeted it.

Without these political developments, post-truth would not have emerged today as a major concern. Most writers who take on the topic mention Trump and Johnson, but neglect the larger political realities that made them possible. To overlook these political developments is to misunderstand post-truth politics. As we shall see, the politics of these tribes, rather than academic epistemological theory, very much drives post-truth and the role of alternative facts. But, at the same time, this is not to overlook an ideological form of epistemic politics through which this politics plays out (Rauch 2018). Insofar as it is a mode of interpretive politics based on competing conceptions of social reality, we can best understand it from the perspective of interpretive social science. To prepare the stage for an interpretive approach to post-truth, however, it is important to distance it from the critiques of postmodernism.

7 Beyond the Critique: Rescuing Interpretive Social Science

Both postmodernism and interpretive social science challenge the objectivist assumptions of positivist policy science. They are not, however, one and the same thing. Further, it should also be pointed out that most of those who try to blame postmodernism for post-truth, despite its problems, exhibit a thin understanding of postmodernism.[5] What is more, there is little direct evidence that post-truth emerged because of postmodernism in one or another of its various forms.

First, it is important to point out that postmodernism is a theoretical orientation that never commanded anything like an established consensus of what it is about, even among its postmodern theorists (Rosenau 1992). While it is true that postmodernism raises fundamental epistemological questions about the constructed nature of knowledge – what is it, and how we get it? – it is also the case that these concerns do not belong to postmodernism per se. From the outset, these have, in fact, been issues in interpretive social science, from Max Weber to Peter Berger, long preceding postmodernism. Moreover, Berger (2006), a founding theorist of contemporary interpretive social science, vehemently rejected postmodernism.[6]

Second, the idea that post-truthers sat around reading postmodern epistemology in order to come up with their political strategies is difficult to verify. That is, it is not as if the radical right post-truthers read postmodern literature and – "aha!" – came up with the idea of post-truth. It is more the case that, for reasons that will be shown later in this work, post-truthers raise their questions about factual knowledge for political reasons, independently of academic epistemological debates.

7.1 The Enlightenment and the Social Construction of Reality

It true that both postmodernists and interpretivists reject the idea of Truth (with a capital "T") and promote, to one degree or another, a relativist understanding of social reality. There have been radical postmodern philosophers who have taken an extremely relativist epistemological position, but there are interpretivists – particularly in the social sciences – who hold a much more moderate understanding of relativism (Rosenau 1992). Moreover, it is important to point out that postmodern-like relativism in general is really not as new as many commentators have implied. Several critics of postmodernism fail to recognize, as John Grey (2017) has put it, that

---

[5] Postmoderism is often employed as a strawman term of derision without much understanding of the philosophy. See here Gibbins and Reimer (1999) and Farkus and Schou (2020:36).

[6] For Berger, a self-identified conservative sociologist, the modern interpretive theory of social constructivism is in no way dependent on or necessarily related to postmodernism.

"modern relativism begins with Enlightenment thinkers." As this distinguished political theorist explains, French Enlightenment philosopher Montesquieu maintained that human values are not culturally fixed. Somewhat later, Marx saw values and worldviews as dependent on their social class origins, and was followed by Mannheim, who recognized that all social knowledge is infused with ideological elements shaped in varying social settings. Thus, in Grey's view, "the postmodern assertion that reality is socially constructed is a footnote to the Enlightenment rather than a departure from it."

7.2 Distrust and the Interpretation of Legitimacy in Turbulent Times

What is more, most fail to recognize that postmodernism is more than just an epistemological orientation. It has also been an intellectual attempt to come to terms with the social and political forces unleashed in society in the 1990s without the help of a preconceived theory. Of particular importance were any number of interconnected factors: "the end of history" debates that emerged after the fall of the Berlin Wall, the rise of identify politics (such as feminism, Black Lives Matter and the LGBTQ movement), the general weakening of social and political structures (resulting from attacks by both the political right and left), the fragmentation and decline of traditional political parties, challenges to scientific expertise and technology, the increase of secularism, the adherence to established religious beliefs, the rise of populist movements and more. Taken as a whole, these phenomena gave rise to a disturbing degree of distrust, a decline in civility and a loss of a cultural sense of "being in it together." Many postmodern theorist have themselves struggled to itemize and understand these complicated social phenomena. Postmodernism, thus, has been as much an attempt to understand a contemporary political and cultural condition as it is a theory of knowledge (Harrison 2004). That is, it seeks to understand the very conditions that have led to post-truth.

Both postmodernism and interpretive social science, it can be argued, have thus been, in significant part, a response to the difficulties of the older conventional epistemologies. Positivism was unable to adequately account for these political phenomena, given the subjective dynamics driving them. Habermas (1975), for example, described the situation as a "legitimacy crisis" confronting positivist scientism. In this respect, one could argue that, in many ways, postmodernism emerged as a response to these knowledge problems, rather than serving as a force to create them (Harrison 2004: 165).

Finally, it can be ironically noted that the charges against postmodernism have largely emerged at the very time when it is seen to be dying (Gibbons 2017).[7] This, however, is not the place to examine the fate of postmodernism. It is enough to say that the criticisms leveled against its theorists – whether right or wrong – divert attention from the essential political factors motivating post-truth. For this reason, we leave a detailed discussion of postmodernism for another time and turn our attention to the potential contribution of an interpretivist epistemology broadly understood. As we will show, an interpretive-based approach, rather than being the source of the problem, has a great deal to offer as a way to understand the post-truth phenomenon generally. Indeed, it can help us understand how post-truth protagonists construct alternative worldviews and the dynamics of post-truth argumentation.

8 The Interpretive Policy-Analytic Approach: Social Meanings and Alternative Realities

An interpretive social-scientific approach to policy inquiry permits us to reinterpret the post-truth issue away from a narrow focus on better facts and toward an understanding of how factual information is processed and understood in social and political contexts (Fischer 2019). It is not that facts, as conventionally understood, are unimportant. Rather, it is that an interpretive perspective focuses attention on the processes of social explanation and argumentation which mediate the understandings of facts in public discourse. And it does so in ways that can help us to both understand and to shape alternative responses that can more effectively address the challenges presented by post-truthers. It is a point that we will illustrate in subsequent sections of the book through an analysis of climate change and COVID-19 denialism.

The starting point for illustrating the role of interpretive social science is the recognition that knowledge is created in the social world, constructed by interacting social actors with differing, often clashing, opinions (Yanow 2000; Rabinow and Sullivan 1987). This is scarcely a new perspective. The interpretive construction of knowledge has roots that trace back to Aristotle and other Greek philosophers. Although there are numerous approaches to interpretivism, it is often attributed in the modern social sciences to Karl Mannheim (1936) and his groundbreaking sociology of knowledge, focused on political thought styles as well as other social phenomenon, including science.

---

[7] If the theory of postmodernism has faded, various concepts associated with postmodernism, such as discourse and narrative, have nonetheless migrated to other disciplines, including policy studies.

Although the interpretivist perspective is now recognized in sociology and political science, it struggled to gain acceptance with many mainstream social scientists, especially those of a positivist persuasion, including those in the policy sciences. But the struggle has not been altogether put to rest, as the post-truth critique of interpretivism shows.

The sociology of knowledge, according to Mannheim, is founded on the idea that both social and scientific theories can in part be traced in significant ways to their social origins as opposed to empirical findings alone. With different emphases, it was an interpretive/constructivist orientation that spread widely in Germany in the 1930s, in England in the 1940s, and in France and the United States in the 1960s. Since the early years of this century, it has played an important role in the critical policy studies movement.

Interpretive social science is geared to understanding the interaction between social meanings and the creation of knowledge – or better, what is taken to be knowledge. As a method of inquiry, it is grounded in the analysis of social meanings in both the everyday social world and in academic expert communities that are themselves a part of that world.[8] In the latter instance, it understands knowledge to be *constructed* by communities of inquirers who measure and construct models of the world, both natural and social, rather than being the product of purely objective observation and analysis. As such, it understands knowledge to be contingent on social traditions, cultural narratives, personal perceptions and experience – the very considerations around which post-truth debates turn.

8.1 Everyday Social Realities and Plausibility Structures

Berger and Luckmann (1965), following the work of Mannheim, emphasized the social constitution of everyday realities. For them, social actors are socialized into "plausibility structures" that involve understandings of how the world works and the ideas that support these views. Relying on the available conceptual structures and narratives, people develop what Berger and Luckmann call a "natural attitude" that provides them with "taken for granted" understandings of social reality.

Through this natural attitude, the phenomena of the social world are taken to be preestablished in schematic patterns that appear to be independent of the social actor's perception and apprehension of events, objects, actions and other occurrences, with the languages employed in the everyday context regularly

---

[8] This study of social meaning in the everyday world draws on the philosophy of phenomenology. The methods of hermeneutics are employed to examine the ways meanings are embedded in texts, actions and artifacts (Yanow and Schartz-Shea 2006).

supplying the objectifications and patterns that make it possible to meaningfully make sense of day-to-day life. It is in this sense that we can understand the way perceptions of reality in the sociopolitical world are often as important as a taken-for-granted conception of reality.

Such social meanings, moreover, are drawn from specific social and societal systems and the worldviews in which they are grounded. The meanings are, in short, part of a larger configuration of social and political narratives that constitute a societal system. Hence, the use of a particular meaning can call forth the larger set of meanings based on different ideas. And, in times like these, it is easy to observe established meanings being called into question by the post-truthers. In this regard, post-truth politics is a politics about social meanings based on alternative conceptions of social reality. Indeed, such political struggles can today be described as a "politics of meaning."

8.2 Scientific Communities in Sociological Perspective

Beyond the everyday life of the citizen, constructivist interpretation pertains to the physical sciences as well. The approach recognizes that scientific communities are organized around competing groups of researchers that can be studied as social groups – the International Panel of Climate Change (IPCC), for example – with theoretical agreement and disagreement often resulting from conflict among expert groups. Although one can argue about the degree of influence of the social components, scientific theories are at any particular point in time partly a byproduct of social and cultural factors. This is a point not well received by many members of the scientific community, but it is based on sociological and historical investigation of real-world scientific practices. Indeed, even if awkwardly so, it is roughly the claim that the climate change deniers make, with positivist scientists taking umbrage. The deniers, however, do not base their claims on history and sociological theory and scientists are not wrong to question the motives of the deniers, as this is about politics rather than scientific judgment. This is a point to which we will return later.

Every object, in this understanding, involves a fusion of physical and social characteristics. Some objects are more physical than social, others are more social than physical. But both dimensions are always present, and one can think of a spectrum ranging from very physical to very social. Whereas the objects of the natural sciences are more physical – such as a tree – the objects of investigation in the social world are more laden with social meaning. The tree, for example, has social meanings about nature attached to it, although most people think of wood and leaves. A woman carries a range of social meanings in society, but can also be treated – and demeaned – as a physical object to satisfy particular masculine needs. Or, to give an example related to post-truth denial, COVID-19 places biological limits on the credibility of particular social meanings. Those who ignore its objective dimensions do so at their own medical peril.

8.3 Societal Institutions and Truth Regimes

The interpretivist understanding of the social world does not only deal with the construction of everyday phenomenological knowledge at a given point in time; it also recognizes that social meanings and the narratives that carry them evolve over time and, as such, are basic to the processes of social and institutional change. Interpretive theory also moves beyond the everyday toward larger social structures that encompass social action, a perspective of particular importance for understanding post-truth arguments.

Writers such as Bourdieu and Foucault have elaborated the interpretive perspective at this level of societal institutions. For Bourdieu, it is necessary to recognize that the meanings of social structures such as schools, hospitals or scientific research institutes are themselves always narratively constructed and interpreted by specific groups of actors – mainly powerful actors – at particular periods of time. These structures are objectified and taken as given in society in general, and act as "objective constraints" through the processes of socialization into the social system, especially through the schooling of new generations. In this way, institutional constraints serve to influence and control the behaviors of the members of a given society. Bourdieu labeled this internalization of the social structure as "habitus." Such constraints, however, can be politicized, as alternative realities emerge and begin to interpret experiences and institutions differently. For example, whereas most citizens accept and respect the medical community for its attention to human health, it becomes possible for populist "anti-vaxxers" to portray medical professionals as a questionable elite seeking to exercise forms of compliance introduced to control the tasks of parenting.

Also focusing on social-structural constraints, Foucault has shown how socially constructed discourses become social constraints reinforced by the dominant institutions – schools, police, social welfare professions and medical institutions, among others – that control the actions of the citizens. Through what he called an "archeology" of societal regimes, focused on how statements and narratives are presented and institutionalized, it becomes possible to uncover the deeper understanding of ideas that a society takes to be truths, or what he called a "regime of truth" – that is, who determines what is taken to be either truth or disinformation.

A truth regime, in Foucault's words, constitutes a "general politics of truth," which specifies the kinds of discourses that are accepted and turned into carriers of what is taken to be truth, the mechanisms that enable people to differentiate true from false claims, the ways in which truth claims are narratively legitimated and sanctioned, the procedures and techniques given value in the quest of truth, and the standing of those responsible for declaring what counts as truth – in short, the very kinds of questions that post-truth climate change and COVID-19 deniers insist on negotiating.

8.4 Multiple Realities as Interpretive Constructions

Constructivism, to be sure, has its critics. The main critique has to do with concerns about relativism, or the idea that all knowledge is only a matter of social perspective. It is a concern that became even more troublesome for many in the latter half of the twentieth century with the emergence of radical forms of postmodernism. Indeed, as already noted, some argue that this relativism is responsible for the emergence of post-truth.

But the criticism often misunderstands the approach, especially as it pertains to the physical world. For the constructivists following theorists such as Mannheim and Berger, it does not mean, as is often assumed, that the world is just a relative creation of the human mind, that there is nothing that is not created by the mind. The fact that social reality is always an interpretive construction created by socially interacting humans, communicatively conveyed through narratives, does not imply that there are no external objects. In fact, one can accept the idea that there is an objective reality to be discovered, but believe it can only be pursued through competing social perspectives.[9] For interpretive social scientists more generally, the categories offered to describe reality are shaped by social relationships and the narrative interactions to which they give rise. The result in the social world, then, is the existence of "multiple realities," or, in the context of the discussion here, what can also be referred to as "alternative realities." In contrast to the commonsense view that takes a particular construct as natural and given, knowledge constructs are thus always partly artifacts of a particular societal system and its sociocultural narratives.

9 Social Meaning in Interpretive Policy Analysis

For interpretive policy analysts, focused on the role of social meanings, policy-making is not a process of rationally planning coherent interventions that tackle

---

[9] This would include the views of many critical realists (Archer et al. 1998).

problems with fixed definitions (van Bommel, van Hulst and Yanow 2020). Contrary to the dominant rational perspective, interpretive policy inquiry, based on a form of "methodological pluralism," examines the "multiple, situated meanings that compete in an effort to define and understand social and political problems" (van Bommel et al. 2020: 71).

Interpretive policy analysis does not deny the importance of empirical data, but it does pose a major epistemological challenge to the positivist approach to policy studies. The traditional positivist modes of policy analysis have largely been unwilling methodologically to include and interpret social meanings. This, as we discussed at the outset, is a result of the principles and practices that dominate the positivist conception of knowledge, in particular the ruling out of attention to the social-subjective side of human life. Specifically, the positivist approach cannot incorporate and account for the social actors' subjective understandings of their situations and actions. Not only is it a general problem for social explanation, but, as we show, it is a special problem when it comes to understanding post-truth politics.

By focusing on the observable dimensions of a social phenomenon, treated as empirical variables, the positivist/empiricist sees the world from a different angle than do their subjects, the positivistic "new narrative policy framework" not withstanding (Jones, McBeth and Shanahan 2014). The models of the empiricists tend, in short, to be influenced by their own implicit assumptions and value judgments, doctrines of scientific neutrality aside. They unwittingly move away from the social-setting context by substituting their own perceptions of the actors' situations and their conceptions of social reality, implicitly if not explicitly. The empiricist's tacit assumptions are usually difficult to uncover as they are often lodged in the structure of their theoretical models. But these are the very same normative assumptions and values that frequently separate the empirical analysts and the post-truth deniers. They are, in fact, operating in different social worlds based on alternative understandings of reality. Only by assuming that one conception of social reality is better than another can one reject the denier's worldview. It is not that this is impossible – indeed, some clearly seem better without much discussion – but in fact these social realities are much more complicated than is usually assumed and thus cannot be summarily rejected by those who merely see the world differently. In any case, as post-truth politics shows, it can only be done at the expense of understanding one another.

9.1 Interpretive Policy Practices

Yanow (2000: 22), the leading theorist of interpretive policy analysis, has outlined the methodological steps of the practice. The first step involves "identifying the language, artifacts, acts and objects" that carry the meanings that compete for attention in the policy process, followed by the task of determining the "communities of meaning" engaged in the effort to define and communicate their interpretations. As in interpretive social science more generally, these meanings are collected through an analysis of discourses, framings, linguistic categories, narratives, arguments, actions and symbolic artifacts (Rabinow and Sullivan 1987). The focus is on how these meanings involve different ways of seeing. This is followed by an effort to locate the particular conflicts surrounding the competing meanings and to elucidate their political implications for policymaking. Finally, the analyst can attempt to mediate the conflicts by negotiating differences across alternative interpretations. This final step, though, is not always required; it depends on the particular interests and purposes of the analyst.

To fully explain a social phenomenon, the interpretive policy analyst thus attempts to grasp the social meanings of the phenomenon from the actor's point of view. That is, the researcher has to enter the social situation of the climate deniers to fully come to grips with their cognitive constructions of reality. In addition to examining the circumstances of the denier's situation and the behaviors associated with them, the interpretation turns on an assessment of these circumstances and behaviors judged against the actor's own motives and values, both stated and imputed. It is at this juncture that we can comprehend the problem that the empiricists have created for themselves. They have methodologically cut themselves off from the information that is needed to engage in a discussion with those who deny particular facts.

The importance of these meanings has been vividly underscored by Schneider and Ingram (2013). As they have demonstrated, public policies are infused with social meanings – positive or negative – for politicians and citizens engaging with fellow members of their communities. They have demonstrated the way policy designs have stories about the understandings pertaining to their target groups built into them, subtly and sometimes not so subtly. These social constructions, constituting multiple realities, are organized around beliefs, stereotypes and images that narratively assign identities to people that connect them to groups that are recipients of beneficial or punitive policies. In populist rhetoric, for example, Mexicans are identified as undeserving criminals surreptitiously sneaking across the border. For Schneider and Ingram, the interpretive-analytic assignment is to uncover these "near-hegemonic" constructions of social reality that often impede democratic policymaking and the processes of social change.

Schuman (1982) has offered a good example of how an interpretivist policy-analytic approach can bring these social meanings into policy analysis. Conducting an interpretive analysis of higher education policy in the United States, he let the students speak for themselves. After reviewing the typical statistically derived explanations that students give to survey researchers about going to college – most of which focus on earning a better living – he showed, through extensive interviews, that such empirical analysis fails to uncover the much more complicated configuration of reasons and motives that students have for going to college, reasons that ultimately shape their final decisions about pursuing an education and thus should also influence the thinking of educational policymakers.

9.2 Interpretation and Social Change

Boltanski (2011) has elaborated this understanding as it relates to social change. For him, the task is to demonstrate how people, laypersons as well as social scientists, participate in processes of meaning creation that lead to social and policy change. He shows the ways that ordinary actors can and do develop and interpret concepts, criteria and narratives through which they are able to construct their own social understandings, policy judgments and even critiques of their situations. Such interpretations by lay people can also challenge policy regulations, as the populist denials of both climate change and COVID-19 show. Such (re)interpretations can be dead wrong, but the formulation of alternative factual understandings has to be understood as part of the social process. In short, objective facts in the sociopolitical world can never be fully separated from the meanings that citizens attach to them.

The social scientist's task is thus not only to supply social actors with top-down social-scientific theories for understanding their situations, but also to comprehend how political and policy actors themselves arrive at and construct their own social understandings, as well as how they experiment with them during their social interactions involving political struggles and policy change. It means that policy researchers need to understand both the sources of the information that lead to such social constructions and the intentions behind their development and spread.

This speaks directly to the problem of coming to grips with those who deny particular facts – namely, to understand the social world in which they are operating and the ways they think in that world. Whereas much of the literature, academic and journalistic, operates on assumptions that privilege scientific knowledge, the post-truthers are motivated by different concerns. Thus, as we have seen, the argument that they are irrational for rejecting expert opinion – which, in a strictly scientific sense, they may well be – only goes so far. It misses a good deal of what we need to know in order to understand their political and policy arguments. For better or worse, they have organized their cognitive worlds in a different way. And it means that they have to be approached on different terms (terms that the deniers can themselves understand). This is a need that takes us into the worldview(s) of the post-truthers in an effort to examine how they construct reality. It is, in short, a task that requires an interpretive social-scientific analysis.

10 Interpretive Social Science and the Scientific Community: The "Hard" Sciences

Given the post-truth attacks on both climate and medical science, it is important to further clarify the constructivist interpretation of scientific knowledge. The scientific community, as we saw, is recognized as a social group (or groups) much like any other social group in society, insofar as it has a status system governed by a hierarchy dedicated to specific practices. Textbook explanations aside, intrinsic here is the view that the theoretical paradigms of scientists and their research communities are partly grounded in the social processes that support them. Scientific disagreements, as research shows, can thus be as much about professional group conflict as they are about formal research conclusions, presented as the products of objective observations based on empirical data. They are, in this regard, influenced by argumentative processes conducted by those deemed to be qualified participants. In this view, knowledge at any point in time is in part a deliberative byproduct of the scientific community and its competing groups of researchers. Up to this point, the explanation does not differ that much from the standard understanding of the process. But what it does not acknowledge or emphasize is that such scientific argumentation can be influenced in significant ways by the location, education and social attitudes of the investigators. Sometimes the influence is only nominal, but at other times it can be important, as climate denial scientists often demonstrate.

10.1 Competing Paradigms

With regard to the hard sciences, the most cited work on constructivism has been Thomas Kuhn's (1962) classic book, *The Structure of Scientific Revolutions*. Perhaps most importantly, this study constituted a confrontational critique by an established scientist of the conventional belief that scientific knowledge moves progressively from hypothesis testing to closer approximations of truth. In a contribution that was at first considered heresy in numerous quarters, Kuhn argued that propositions about reality are rooted in theoretical paradigms. Providing a conceptual understanding of the research subject, a theoretical approach and a set of methodological practices, paradigms put forth by competing scientific groups supply the lens through which empirical findings are made to make sense.

Progress in science, then, is for Kuhn a movement from a less to a more accurate paradigm. Empirical results from one paradigm will most likely be incommensurate with those of another paradigm. The research process is driven by data that cannot be adequately understood outside a given paradigm. As anomalous findings mount, there may be a search for a new paradigm to better explain it. As Kuhn explains, the scientist with an alternative framework comes to see the problem and its solutions differently. Major scientific progress thus emerges from a shift in paradigms, rather than a continuous building of results within the dominant paradigm. In this way, as he made clear, it becomes necessary to rethink the traditional notion of objective truth.

10.2 Interpretive Communities

Such work underscores the role of "interpretive communities" in the assessment of the objective realities most scientists accept at any particular time. But this does not mean that scientific findings are only interpretations. Other scholars who have followed up on this tradition have focused on scientific knowledge as a more complicated product of relational processes that involves the communicative interchanges of the scientists engaged in the research, the physical settings of the research and the objects of investigation themselves. As Latour and Woolgar (1986) explain in their study of "laboratory life," scientists are thus not to be understood as the pawns of a process driven by social factors, but rather as interacting participants in complex physical and social interpretations that produce commonly accepted knowledge.

Scientists, however, do exercise their preferences and interests along the way: the Nobel Prize winner typically resists findings that suggest his or her work needs to be abandoned thanks to a new paradigm. That is, as interpretive communities, scientific groups can and do act like other social groups organized around interests, motives and hierarchies, as a good deal of history and sociology of science has shown.

10.3 Coproduction of Knowledge

One of the most prominent approaches of the social construction of scientific knowledge today is Jasanoff's (2004) theory of the coproduction of science, a theory that sees public science as a fusion of society and scientific research. Coproduction, as she puts it, rests on the basic contention that the way we come to know and portray the world, both natural and societal, are inherently related to the way we decide to inhabit it. In this understanding, the scientific community is influenced by norms and institutions narratively constructed by the state. The knowledge produced by this science can be biased by the political intentions for conducting it and particular understandings of the objects of investigation. It also means that such science generally serves – indirectly and directly – to legitimate a truth regime's understandings of the objects, however partial, and thus typically rests on implicit sociopolitical narratives that support the dominant power structures.

11 Citizens Confront the Experts: Context and Emotion in Ordinary Reason

How, then, do citizens in the everyday life-world respond to the knowledge put forward by scientific experts? To understand this we need to compare the ordinary knowledge of the citizen with the knowledge of the scientist. Toward this end, we have to recognize the ways in which the citizens' knowledge is forged in their everyday social context rather than handed down by social scientists and other experts. This is especially important to understand in the case of post-truth politics. Often presented as commonsense wisdom, in public affairs it can at times trump the complex knowledge offered by expert communities, which is much more difficult for ordinary citizens to comprehend. Given that post-truth explicitly questions or rejects scientific knowledge, it is essential to understand the tensions between these two forms of knowledge.

It hardly needs to be said that scientific reason is widely considered to be the superior form of knowledge. Ordinary commonsense knowledge, however, can itself be seen as an alternative form of knowledge that has its place in public controversies. One important reason for this is the fact that science often cannot adequately supply the knowledge necessary to make solid or irrefutable policy decisions – or, at least, not enough of it. Policymakers must frequently make decisions that address urgent problems before scientifically validated findings can be made available. In such cases, citizens rely on their stock of social and experiential knowledge (Lindblom and Cohen 1979).

11.1 Scientific versus Sociocultural Reason

We understand these two forms of knowledge to be organized around different modes of reason and rationality (Diesing 1962). Whereas scientific knowledge is laid out formally in the philosophical and methodological texts that rigorously spell out its methods, ordinary everyday rationality is organized around sociocultural reason. It is not that the world of social and political affairs ordinarily ignores scientific knowledge; rather, it's that reason in the social realm follows a different logic or rationality. While scientific reason puts its faith in the rational application of empirical methods and evidence, the sociocultural reason of the citizen is generally geared toward interactions grounded in social and political contexts rather than decontextualized technical calculations (Fischer 2005).

Stressing the opinions of traditional sociopolitical elites and personal peer groups, sociocultural rationality tends to trust social process over scientific outcomes or quantifiable impacts (Plough and Krimsky 1987). As knowledge tied to social group membership, Mannheim referred to it as "essentially connected knowledge" (*Seinverbundenes Wissen*). It is not that scientific data is irrelevant, but rather that it is processed in the social contexts to which it relates or is applied – that is, the contexts in which it is to have an impact. People identifying with a populist movement will thus process information about COVID-19 within a different situational context than the head of a virology department.

Beyond the data, then, people's perceptions are interpreted in the context of the circumstances surrounding the identification, the problem, the place or standing of the people in their community who make it known, and the values and social traditions of the community as a whole. It processes the impacts, intrusions or implications of particular events, phenomena or technical artifacts on the social and political relations of that world (Fischer 2005).

11.2 Social Cognition and Affective Factors

For the actors, the issues are interpreted as much in terms of qualitative, affective factors as they are in terms of empirical relationships. The interpretative social scientist understands real-world events to be made up of a rich and multifaceted set of factors, of which empirical data is only one part. Indeed, it is a perspective well suited to understanding technically oriented policy controversies, such as climate change or medical concerns such as COVID-19. For example, research related to environmental risk shows that citizens' understandings are influenced by basic categorical dichotomies such as their familiarity (or otherwise) with the people involved, who controls the risky events, whether they are produced by natural or artificial forces, the immediacy or delayedness of potential effects and the visibility or invisibility of the benefits and costs (Slovic 1979). According to such research, people process information, especially uncertain information, in terms of previous experiences pertinent to such assessments (Plough and Krimsky 1987). According to this social process theory of cognition (Nurius 2013), they deal with such uncertainties by drawing on familiar, trusted knowledge to fill in the information gaps (Fischer 2005).

Some people, for example, will assess the perceived threat of COVID-19 by filling the information gaps with knowledge of their experiences with the influenza that arrives every year when the weather turns cold. This is also the case when competing interests exploit uncertain data by emphasizing different interpretations of the findings. In these cases, activists and politicians attempt to fill the gap with arguments related to the definition of the problem itself.

11.3 Reason, Mistrust and Emotional Outrage

These knowledge issues are particularly relevant when decisions are rendered by anonymous and distant organizations. For instance, people want to learn why and how climate policy decisions were made, which interests are involved, whether a hidden agenda is behind them, who is responsible for it, whether there are protections if things go wrong, and so forth (Fischer 2005). When people have experiences that indicate they should be distrustful of public officials, experiential evidence can override empirical findings (Fischer 2005). Indeed, from environmental risk research we learn that when worries run high, an emotionally laden phenomenon psychologists refer to as the "dread" or "outrage" factor can emerge. If mistrust and hostility run out of control, giving rise to highly emotional political reactions, the uncertainties of the empirical risks tend to be amplified (Sandman 1987). In the case of COVID-19, distrust of government officials has led to outrage expressed at demonstrations around the world.

12 Political and Policy Knowledge as Ordinary Practical Knowledge

Many scientists and technical experts have long held citizens' responses to be irrational, just as in the cases of climate, vaccine and COVID-19 denial. Indeed, there is a long tradition of positivist thought that points to such "irrationalities" and maintains that ordinary social knowledge cannot be considered valid knowledge. While this can seem true from a rigorous scientific perspective, it misunderstands the nature of social knowledge, including its political variant. As Mannheim (1936: 164–191) made clear, sociopolitical knowledge is structured differently than forms of physical knowledge, and it employs its own logic of inquiry. Whereas physical science is objective/empirical in nature, sociopolitical knowledge is a normative construction that has to be judged by its own evaluative criteria (Scriven 1987).

Unlike the positivist approach to scientific knowledge, which strives for empirical impartiality, such sociopolitical knowledge, focused on social meanings, is a normative fusion of ideas, values, factual information, situational circumstances, probable consequences and political interests. Often bound together by emotional convictions, this sociopolitical fusion is thus inherently interpretive, but not irrational as the term is normally understood. As Mannheim

(1936: 173) put it, whereas "the scientist always approaches his subject matter with an ordering and schematizing tendency," the social or political actor "seeks orientation with reference to action" to be taken in concrete social situations. This leads the political actor to interpret the meaning of actions in terms of their real-world life contexts. In the light of available knowledge about political processes, political actors focus on strategic courses of action designed to support or change a situation within the larger societal structures of which they are a part and the value commitments inherent to them. As such, they forge a middle course between social and political ideas related to action and the immediate practical context of assumptions, meanings and feelings in which an action-oriented decision has to apply. Political knowledge – including such knowledge as cognitively processed by post-truthers – is thus an interpretive construction guided by ideas and values, but shaped by and adapted to the pragmatic empirical and normative realities of the action-oriented situation. This includes people who hold political views based on disinformation.

12.1 Political Knowledge and the Levels of Policy Argumentation

Political knowledge, whether ideologically or policy-oriented, is a mode of practical reason concerned with the normative question of "what ought to be done" (Fischer 2003). Borrowing from the constructivist-oriented "ordinary language philosophers" of practical reason (Taylor 1961; Toulmin 1958), one can recognize policy evaluation to be a form of thought that interpretively involves a techno-empirical evaluation of a proposed course of action (e.g., climate change data) to a consideration of the specific contextual factors to which the action would apply (e.g., parts of the country on the coastlines), then to an interpretation of its implications for the societal system (e.g., decline of economic growth), followed by an assessment of the principles and values (e.g., health, freedom, social welfare, and the like) embedded in the social system (Taylor 1961; Fischer 1995, 2007). This probe, then, involves an interpretive interaction between relevant empirical and normative criteria. In a deliberation about a particular policy topic, different actors will focus on different levels of analysis. Some will interpret the core of the problem to be at the technical level (environmental engineers), while others will believe it to be lodged in the larger societal system (climate deniers worried about the implications of environmental regulations). All levels, however, remain present and potentially relevant, even if tacitly so, and can be called forward any time the participants find it justified to do so, sometimes motivated by passionate convictions. Although less rigorous than scientific logic, practically oriented sociocultural reason is nonetheless organized around an "informal logic" with its own rules and structures (Taylor 1961; Fischer 1995).

12.2 Interpreting Validity in Practical Reason

From this perspective, we can see that the validity of any practical claim for a participant depends in important ways on its relationship to a conception of core beliefs basic to a particular understanding of the good society. That is, knowledge that does not contribute to a move in a particular ideological direction, while possibly empirically valid, is seen to be either irrelevant, of no interest or problematic. Sociocultural practical reason need not challenge the empirical data per se, but it does determine the degree to which it will be considered important for, or relevant to, a particular course of action. Often lost in the political debates about climate change data, including the passionate politics of climate denial, are the political implications of this mode of reason for policy decisions. This is a point that will be illustrated in the case of both climate and COVID-19 denial argumentation.

Insofar as all public action-oriented knowledge is grounded in politics, one way or another, policymaking and thus policy knowledge are also fundamentally political, despite attempts by technocratic experts and policymakers to conceal this reality from view. Policy knowledge, like politically oriented knowledge more generally, can be understood as a normative construction designed to address – call for, support and justify – decisions about specific courses of action in political processes (as opposed to political-science knowledge about the working of political processes). As Mannheim (1936: 164–191) explained, unlike scientists generally, the political actor "seeks orientation with reference to action" to be taken in concrete situations. This leads the political actor to first view things in social terms relevant to the real-world life contexts of which they are a part, and, second, after considering the available knowledge about political processes – both expert and experiential – to offer a strategic course of policy actions. The actions are designed to support or change a specific situation in light of the larger sociopolitical structures of which they are a part and the value commitments inherent to them. The resulting decisions are also generally influenced by the emotional commitments attached to these elements, adding varying measures of intensity to both political and policy deliberations.

12.3 Political Thought Styles in Policymaking

Grounded in an ideological orientation, knowledge for policy politics is attached to a set of beliefs about what is good for both the individual actor and society more generally, in both the short and long runs.[10] Such knowledge

---

[10] Sabatier (1988) theorized the role of core beliefs in policy belief systems.

typically rests on ideas about how the world works, how it should work and the appropriate strategy for change. Over time, political and policy struggles around competing ideologies give rise to what Mannheim (1936) called "thought styles." A thought style refers to "a socially constructed ordering of arguments that is traceable back to a specific social group and its social quest to influence the public interpretation of reality" (Lundberg 2013). Competing styles of thought approach the disputes with different assumptions and premises (Mannheim 1936: 147), which helps us to understand why political groups have trouble reaching consensus in policy disputes. Such groups, as Mannheim wrote (1986:55), do more than strive to achieve their particular economic interests; they also seek to create and inhabit a world in which they feel they can belong. In this regard, the concept also captures the populist post-truth thought style that not only questions the role of expert facts, but also involves a search for a social and political home to which they feel they can belong (Gitlin 2020). It is a search that is expressed with emotional passion, giving the struggle the "feel" of truth, as a kind of gut assessment that their ideas "ring true."

Further, policy politics is also as much about creating new realities as it is about sustaining existing realities. In this regard, what are generally referred to as the existing social and political facts – the stuff of the experts – need not always be considered entirely relevant, as the goal can to be create new realities.

13 Climate Policy and Denialism: A Political Illustration

Understanding the construction of political knowledge thus helps us explain a policy problem that otherwise constitutes one of the perplexingly irrational issues of our time. How can people deny a coming climate crisis in the face of the empirical facts? The answer requires an examination of the everyday "plausibility structures" of these deniers.

The starting point for such an analysis is the recognition that climate denial, embedded in the politics of the radical right-wing movements which have swept across many Western countries, has created a divisive politics that has created major problems for meaningful climate deliberations. Indeed, in the United States this right-wing politics led Trump to signal withdrawal from the Paris Climate Accord, supported and encouraged by the climate denial of his first anti-environmental Environmental Protection Agency Administrator (a born-again right-wing lawyer who went out his way to both fire and silence governmental climate scientists). With some 97 percent of the scientific community agreeing that human activities are a major factor contributing to current levels of climate change, this has more than baffled a large swath of the global environmental community. Although typically written off as an irrational exercise in know-nothing politics, we can find an alternative explanation by turning to the social dimensions related to the facts that deniers place in question.

13.1 Sociopolitical Meanings Rather than Climate Findings

From a closer examination of the arguments of climate deniers, generally supported by a vast array of conservative think tanks (Dunlap and Jacques 2013), we can glean the reality that, despite appearances to the contrary, the basic concern is not about facts per se (or what the deniers see as the information presented as the facts); rather, it is about the meanings attached to them. As part of a political camp that regards anything the "other side" says with extreme skepticism, climate deniers simply reject the findings of climate researchers based on what they see to be the motives behind their studies. That is, what they reject more than the data is what they see to be the social-political dynamics that have generated it. For them, the concern is about the norms and values the research supports.

The data, according to the conservative deniers, is the product of a liberal political system that governs a social life-world they distrust and reject. Living in an alternative social life-world to the one inhabited by liberal climate environmentalists, the members of this group believe the world to be directed by a set of cosmopolitan elites – including a liberal urban intelligentsia – that are a danger to their own way of life. Taking the existing global system to be an evil construction engineered by these political elites and the scientists that serve them, many of them see such experts as part of a conspiracy. Indeed, they largely take the expert communities and the universities that train them to be bastions of left-leaning liberalism – or socialism – promoting big government and its regulatory truth regime. So intense is this worry that they feel an urgent and justified need to oppose and block this political effort at every turn. In fact, this stance is often so extreme that it can best be described in terms of dread and outrage. Such climate deniers are sufficiently emotionally exercised by the current state of affairs that their reactions can be understood in terms of the "outrage factor" identified by environmental research.

13.2 The IPCC as an Epistemic Regime

From this perspective, it is not difficult for these conservatives to believe that the IPCC's climate experts, employed by those said to be advancing a surreptitious global conspiracy, are personally and politically biased. In this argument, climate experts are portrayed as a social group with particular interests, including funding and institutional support from the United Nations, geared toward advancing the power and influence of their own hierarchies and the methodological procedures that guide them. Although climate deniers do not derive their critique from the theory of regime truth, they arrive at the same or similar conclusions from their own perspective, which, in important ways, is a test of the theory (Fuller 2018). If this in fact involves a liberal epistemic or truth regime, it would then not be surprising to learn that the climate deniers want to question the findings of the IPCC, which they do.

What they do, in the face of these extreme worries coupled with heightened distrust, is feed their sense of uncertainty with sociocultural ideas forged in their long, ongoing struggle with political liberals. It is thus as much about the kinds of people they take liberals to be as it is about political liberalism. Under normal political conditions there could be room for considering the data on its own terms before accepting or rejecting it. But under conditions of high-level emotionally charged distrust, the deniers are unwilling to enter into a rational discourse with scientific experts. Without reference to the theory of social construction, conservatives can on their own come to suspect or believe that the experts might be selectively constructing – e.g., "cherry-picking" – the data, to one degree or another, infusing them with their own personal, political and social biases. In the extreme, they rhetorically describe the presentation of these biased facts as "fake news."

This can be taken as a cynical or self-serving strategic strategy; but, from an interpretive perspective, it can also be understood as a construction of climate knowledge, in ways that correspond to the constructivist understanding of knowledge in general. For the deniers, this construction of climate knowledge is then attributed to the liberal environmental political biases of climate scientists and activists.

13.3 Alternative Facts and the Future of Capitalism

There is good evidence of this in Klein's (2011) investigation of the sixth annual climate conference at the Heartland Institute, the primary organization of the deniers.[11] The scientific findings, as she determined, were not the main worry organizing their talks. Speakers spoke more about policies to combat global warming that they see as "an attack on middle-class American capitalism." Climate change, it was argued, is less concerned about the state of the environment and has more to do with "shackling capitalism and transforming the American way of life in the interests of global wealth redistribution." As Delingpole argued, "modern environmentalism successfully advances many of the causes dear to the left: redistribution of wealth, higher taxes, greater

---

[11] The discussions in Sections 13.3, 14 and 15 appeared in Fischer (2019) and are reproduced with permission.

government intervention, and regulation" (cited in Klein 2011). And Bast, the president of the institute, adds that climate change is, for the political left, "the perfect thing . . . It's the reason why we should do everything [the left] wanted to do anyway" (Klein 2011).

Here, we clearly encounter the political paranoia of these right-wing deniers (Fischer 2019). They fear "this entire environmental movement simply as a green Trojan horse" and "a plot to steal American freedom" (Fischer 2019). Some go even further, arguing that the IPCC climate scientists are the functionaries of a dangerous and hidden cabal of "deep state" subversives made up of Democrats, intelligence community members, high-level global officials and numerous celebrities, among other nefarious elites – that is, the very same people that Trump regularly rails against.

The first step of these environmentalists, as Horner argues (quoted in Klein 2011), is to remove the "nagging freedoms" that both get in the way of climate change policy and can also serve as a pretext for imposing their own political values. What "free society," he asks, "would do to itself what this agenda requires" (Klein 2011)? As another key speaker argued, climate change data is actually not the real and pressing issue, leading Klein (2011) to realize that "it isn't the message at all." Rather, their message is that the revered ideas and values of American culture are under frontal attack and in serious jeopardy.

For people who think that the most important goal is "freeing people from the tyranny of other people," it can begin to look like the demise of the world. "When we look at this issue," as Bast argues (in Klein 2011), "this is a recipe for massive increase in government . . . Before we take this step, let's take another look at the science. So conservative and libertarian groups, I think, stopped and said, let's not simply accept this as an article of faith; let's actually do our own research," calling for the proper use of scientific procedures (Klein 2011). Klein takes this to mean that it is not an explicit or primary "opposition to the scientific facts of climate change that drives denialists but rather opposition to the real-world implications of those facts."

And while it is not the end of the world as such, it does spell the demise of *their* world in most ways, real or imagined. As Klein puts it, "climate change detonates the ideological scaffolding on which contemporary conservatism rests." In no way can a core belief system that "vilifies collective action and venerates total market freedom" be reconciled "with a problem that demands collective action on an unprecedented scale." Such action calls for a "dramatic reining in of the free market forces," seen by most environmentalists as having brought about the ecological crisis.

Klein (2011) concludes with a message for the political left. As she puts it, " when it comes to the real-world consequences of those scientific findings, specifically the kind of deep changes required not just to our energy consumption but to the underlying logic of our economic system, the crowd gathered at the Marriott Hotel may be in considerably less denial than a lot of professional environmentalists," or at least than "the ones who paint a picture of global warming Armageddon, then assure us that we can avert catastrophe by buying 'green' products and creating clever markets in pollution."

For the climate deniers, then, the concern about a political-economic way of life constitutes the alternative perspective that for them is the priority issue. As such, it necessitates attention to a different set of considerations and facts pertinent to their concerns – alternative facts – related to protecting their own ideological orientation and the way of life that it supports. It need not be that the IPCC research is necessarily false, but rather that it is not the primary worry for them, especially as they recognize the implications of the numbers. In their view, an alternative fact is the destruction of individual freedom and the free-market system. As one fellow put it, let's be absolutely sure about the evidence before we jeopardize our values. Here, being sure means making certain that they can trust the scientists that have produced these numbers. Who are these people? What are their political beliefs? Can they be trusted? And so on.

These are questions drawn from their own stock of social beliefs – which is knowledge, for them – about an ongoing global liberal politics that employs scientific experts, paid for by the United Nations, which many of them see to be a very troublesome (dangerous, even) institution that is up to nothing good (Klein 2005).[12] Others in this "stealth organization" are seen to be interested in overtaking the United States in the name of a questionable program called sustainable development.

14 Climate Policy and Politics: The Social Translation of Evidence into Political Knowledge

What does it mean, more specifically, to say that climate deniers focus on the social and political meanings of the evidence? What they recognize, explicitly or implicitly, is that empirical findings in the political world have to be translated into "political knowledge" (Fischer 2019). More specifically, policy-related evidence has to be translated into knowledge that fits into the relevant political narrative, or at least can interpretively accommodate it. Indeed, this is how Allen (2017) described the role of the IPCC itself in the climate discourse of the 1990s.

---

[12] The point is captured by John Bolton, Trump's former National Security Advisor, who once said the top 10 ten floors of the UN executive offices could be lopped off and nobody would notice the difference (Klein 2005).

14.1 The Interpretive Grammar of Climate Security

Although climate change is generally presented in terms of relatively straight-forward numbers that indicate degrees of warming, Allen (2017) shows how the numbers can be interpreted to carry a political message when they enter policy debates. As he explains, climate change in the early years of the debate was presented as an existential issue of environmental risk, but was later extended to be interpreted as a matter of national security. The data was first translated by environmentalists into a form of political knowledge that sought to portray the numbers as if they implied a fundamental threat to humankind, even its survival. Later, he argues, scientists and political leaders adopted "the grammar of security" to strengthen the argument that climate change is a threat to life on the planet. That is, rather than just putting out the data, they sought to motivate political change by interpretively connecting the data to ideas about technology, the history of the earth and humankind's place on it. These narratives, moreover, often offered dramatic – even, at times, draconian – policy recommendations related to carbon emission reductions, sharp transitions to new and more efficient forms of energy, and massive investments in climate-related research and the development of new technologies. A global security risk, in short, was espoused as "a vision of natural order that made clear the necessity for, and possibility of, a global politics of climate" (Miller 2004: 55). Constructed independently of new and more compelling data, these narratives supplied sociopolitical frames into which the data was fitted and presented to the public.

14.2 Political Facts

In this view, climate change research was as much a matter of how to get it on the political agenda as it was of collecting the relevant numbers presented as the facts that need to be faced. This is in contrast to the school of environmental theorists who argue that prominent climate scientists came to constitute an epistemic community that won the day with empirical findings (Haas 1989). Allen shows how this community of experts strategically employed their scientific consensus to help the international political community to put climate-related action on the political agenda. He reveals how leading scientists often did more than marshal data; they sought to politicize it by interpretively framing it as an issue of environmental security and human survival – that is, ideas that the data itself does not inherently carry. They used scientific knowledge – subtly and not so subtly – to focus political attention on the need for particular kinds of societal transformations. As Franz (1997) put it, it was an effort "to transform scientific facts into political facts." Rather than just putting forward scientific and technical research findings, they embedded them in larger Cold War narratives about the roles of scientific technologies and catastrophic threats (Edwards 2010).

For climate deniers, this is portrayed as a scare tactic perpetuated by a truth regime made up of climate scientists, politicians and bureaucrats. As we saw, some go even further, arguing that they are the functionaries of "deep state" subversives. Bast and his colleagues implicitly understand that climate policy science in the public sphere is a social construction that fuses empirical findings with social and political meanings. Without spelling it out theoretically, they recognize the coproduction of climate science – namely, that the way people interpret and present the world is inseparably shaped by the way they choose to live in it. Scientific research, in this way, is organized around a set of norms and values supported by state institutions that constitutes an "epistemic regime" supportive of a given way of life (Rauch 2021).

It is in this sense that the climate deniers are not entirely wrong to argue that the climate science placed in the public realm is related to political strategy. They correctly recognize that the societal implications are big, but they are seldom spelled out or publicly discussed – that is, the potential need for a planned society, a greater role for experts and restraints on individual freedoms.

15 Climate Research: Uncertain Knowledge and Falsification

Leading deniers do not necessarily reject science. Indeed, many are too clever to wander into this epistemological deadend. More typically, they say that it is important to get both the scientific evidence and political priorities right. As Bast put it to his Heartland Institute colleagues, before accepting the recommendations of the IPCC – given that its findings are seen to involve a massive increase in government at the expense of freedom – conservatives and libertarians should not just accept the findings; they should promote research of their own, he argues (cited in Klein 2011). The Institute takes it a step further, calling for a "restoration of the scientific method," by which its members mean unbiased research they can trust. And here they are not without supportive arguments. Indeed, they can appeal to sophisticated theories of knowledge. Pointing to Popper's theory of falsification, for example, they have emphasized that scientific results need to be regularly subjected to contestation and refutation. Climate skeptic Stewart Franks (2014), appealing to the well-established epistemological canon of independent empirical verification, argues that much of the public information about climate change cannot in fact withstand Poppers's test of falsification.

Although one could find this disingenuous, given the existing consensus based on the research of leading climate scientists, climate deniers can nonetheless argue that IPCC scientists have not *proven* their case. It is a challenge that can be easily deployed by those who wish to oppose a policy based on the evidence. And it can be done with a straight face, as it is not altogether wrong: the issue has not been "proven," a point that can resonate with many of those who rely on the standard understanding of scientific investigation held by most people. Climate skeptics can say with justification that the causes of climate change, especially the human role, have not been *proven* in any final way and call for further research upon which to base firm policy decisions. They can do it, moreover, by citing a number of reputable climate scientists who assert, correctly, that many questions related to global warming have not been settled.

It is just here that interpretive policy inquiry can offer an essential insight. According to the approach, as we have seen, that which is taken to be knowledge at any one point in time is a matter of scientific consensus – that is, consensus among the qualified members of the relevant community. And this is what the community of climate scientists have offered: a consensus based on existing peer-reviewed research. Indeed, it is what constructivism expects them to do; it can, in fact, be support for the theory.

15.1 From Uncertain Knowledge to Biased Scientists

A newer wave of climate deniers, however, has moved beyond questioning the data to focus on the construction of specific climate arguments, in part because they have been losing the data battle. Many of these deniers have come to more or less accept the scientific consensus about the human contribution to warming and have shifted to an argument that the problem is too big to be able to do anything to mitigate or adapt to the consequences. Moreover, whatever might be done is seen to have a drastic impact on the economy (Demelle 2017; Lomborg 2001). For them, the risks are too great given our limited knowledge about climate change and how to deal with it. Countries could pour huge amounts of money into mitigation and adaption and still fail to bring the problem under control.

In addition, some deniers, rather than challenge the findings per se, have chosen to politically smear climate change activists and scientists as biased. Cann and Raymond (2018) discover this trend to be growing, replacing to a degree the emphasis on uncertain data. Focusing on particular scientists, they portray their work as "flawed and biased," likening some to "heretics" and even "Nazi sympathizers." Indeed, such denigration is a standard strategy of post-truth politics generally.

15.2 Climategate

One of the most notable efforts along these lines was the hacking of the email accounts of climate researchers at East Anglia University in the UK, one of the leading climate research universities (Pappas 2011). To the great embarrassment of the climate science community, they pointed to some 5,000 hacked emails stolen from the climate scientists at East Anglia University in the UK and posted on a Russian server. In some of these emails leading researchers spoke of the need to organize and present the climate data in the strongest possible terms. In fact, there was even a suggestion of "spinning" the message. Insofar as they were accused of massaging the evidence pertaining to the human contribution to climate warming just before the Copenhagen Environmental Summit, the press took up the issue and spoke of "climategate." One email writer, for example, wrote that he "cannot overstate the HUGE amount of political interest in the project as a message that the government can give on climate change to help them tell their story." He added that "they want their story to be a very strong one and don't want to be made to look foolish" (Waugh 2011). Worse, another discussed the advisability of hiding or obscuring findings that didn't fit the standard climate change scenario. This led climate skeptics and deniers to express outrage about the findings of biased scientists. They insisted that climate policy decisions should be based on all of the available evidence, including findings that did not suit the biases of IPCC climate experts, a position that, on the surface, sounded responsible.

This proved to be more than a little awkward to the scientists involved, leading to investigations by the university. As such, it was raw meat for the conservative social media. But what it actually did, from the interpretive perspective presented here, was to confirm the constructivist understanding of the scientific work. The scientific community was seen to constitute a social group – with all of the typical human foibles – that involves individual scientists with opinions based on their beliefs and values. This did not, as claimed, refute the data as such; it actually illustrated the human dimension of an epistemic community, as well as demonstrating the interpretive nature of strategic policy argumentation when science is presented for use in political decision-making. It is the same political translation process that Allen has described. All sides do it, but they try to hide behind conventional understandings of science when they present their work.

The climate change illustration shows, then, that better facts and fact-checking will not dissuade the deniers. They are essentially concerned with the political and social meanings attached to the climate data rather than the empirical evidence per se. We turn at this point to an examination of the construction of policy arguments related to COVID-19 denial. Here, the focus is on ways in which social meanings are used to counter or deflect fact-based COVID-19 policy arguments.

16 COVID-19 Denialism: Interpreting Narrative Arguments

The denial or downplaying of COVID-19 is also an important illustration of post-truth politics. In this section, we turn to post-truth denial narratives and the COVID-19 counterarguments drawn from them. As MacIntyre (2007) has written, when people take up the question of "what should to be done," they typically give answers that begin with a narrative story. Following suite, most COVID-19 deniers offer a narrative that carries the normative and empirical assumptions upon which their arguments are constructed (or "narrative arguments").

COVID-19 deniers, like climate deniers, ground their arguments in narratives about the workings of the society and its political system. Typically, it is a radically conservative story of decline at the hands of liberal elites, both politicians and experts. In the United States it is by and large the "Make America Great Again" narrative intrinsic to Donald Trump's political rhetoric. In Britain, a version of the same conservative narrative is found among the "Brexiteers" dedicated to returning the country to its former greatness.

For COVID-19 deniers, the policy measures to combat the virus, as advocated by central government health authorities in the United States, are seen to be a threat to basic American values, freedom and individualism, just as is the case with climate change. There is no single version of the COVID-19 denial narrative as it is expressed in several different ways, with various plots and subplots. It involves, however, two primary narratives from which deniers draw heavily to defend their arguments, one being an anti-science narrative and the other involving a "deep state" conspiracy story. While elements of these two narratives are often intermeshed, the general issues of these two storylines can be sufficiently differentiated for the present purposes (Krugman 2020). Moreover, the denial narratives and arguments often overlap with or include claims made by less radical COVID-19 skeptics, such as those mostly worried about scientific reliability of the expertise. The hardcore denialists, in contrast, shift to a much deeper – often conspiracy-oriented – sociopolitical critique of societal lockdown and its related policy measures. In this regard, as we shall see, the deniers' narrative argument can be understood to operate at two levels of policy argumentation.

Like skeptics, the deniers tend to share concerns about uncertain and conflicting information, though often for different reasons. Their stories easily align with genuine disagreements related to specific scientific issues, statistical reporting in particular. In terms of the efforts to understand the virus, it is possible to discuss and challenge factual information related to COVID-19 on its own terms. Indeed, there are considerations presented by those within the scientific community that can at some points justify, or appear to justify, genuine skepticism. For one thing, deniers – like skeptics – can easily discern a degree of disagreement among the experts. This is especially the case regarding statistics pertaining to infections. For example, as discussed later, the way this data is calculated and presented can leave room for misunderstanding and controversy.

16.1 COVID-19 Policy: Bureaucratic Missteps

There have also been programmatic missteps and informational errors of various sorts that have become part of the denial argument. Information provided to the public about wearing protective face masks and social distancing was often unclear, especially at the outset. Often deniers relate these failures to big, liberal-style bureaucratic government, as well as to an animosity toward global institutions, the World Health Organization (WHO) in particular. Failures on the part of the WHO provided openings for Trump to attack it as incompetent, calling for a withdrawal of US financial support. This critique is part of a narrative argument supported by the more general conservative attack on international organizations that preceded the emergence of COVID-19. These disagreements and errors were easily woven into the larger denial narrative, further opening the door for a significant measure of distrust, especially among those already looking for ways to confirm their worries and doubts about bloated bureaucratic systems managed by unrepresentative technocrats. While most deniers cannot credibly muster the analytical capabilities to challenge empirical errors related to the various pandemic policy measures, there are conservative experts ready to help them do that, albeit some with questionable intentions in mind.

A careful look shows that it is often not that the experts' statistics are necessarily wrong, but rather a matter of who is offering them and why. The denier's storylines, in this regard, are generally based on the belief that the numbers can be slanted in ways to emphasize one interpretation over another, justifying a degree of skepticism until proven otherwise.

16.2 Anti-Science Narratives

In additional to the deniers' argument about problematic information, a second major argument is lodged in an anti-science narrative portraying most of the COVID-19 experts as presenting statistics that harbor a liberal political bias, despite their claims to scientific truth and value neutrality. This is an antipathy similar to that which we find in climate denial, but in this case the COVID-19 denial narrative is often also connected to the anti-vaccination movement, or "anti-vaxxers" (Ball 2020). It is, as such, linked to a mindset that questions the wisdom of getting vaccinated, frequently embracing medicines and treatments that have never been proven (Anderson 2020). The argument is part of a deeper conservative narrative that elevates the "common sense" of the ordinary citizen over government experts, pointing to a medical profession that prescribes medicines without adequately considering the needs of their patients.

One finds this storyline running through the right-wing media. Both so-called "liberal experts" and a "liberally biased media" in the United States are accused of promoting their own interpretations of events as opposed to those of others, with the intent of making the Trump administration look bad. Many of the deniers have even described the COVID-19 statistics as part of a political narrative designed to bring down the Trump administration (Arantani 2020).

This critique of science and expertise is also facilitated by the fact that other experts, largely featured in the conservative media, do offer different statistical numbers on infection rates. One argument that some of them advance is the contention that COVID-19 is no more dangerous than the ordinary flu, which also kills large numbers of people each year. Others point to the fact the vast majority of those who fall ill survive the virus, a point they say is underplayed by the establishment media. They also argue that higher infection rates only reflect increases in the rates of testing: the numbers rise because more people are tested rather than because more people are becoming infected. Some contend that the measurement of infections and deaths from COVID-19 are based on outdated epidemiological techniques designed for a different kind of disease. Such criticisms, taken together, led the director of the Center for Disease Control's mortality statistics research to concede that the situation is so "politically charged" that people look for excuses to question the statistics (Schoenfeld, Jones and Gamio 2020).

Further, some claim that the scientific experts engage in COVID-19 research because it offers large amounts of research monies for their state-funded laboratories, along with the possibility of gaining public notoriety. As something of a hidden plot, scientific experts are thus said to be more interested in themselves than in the general well-being of ordinary citizens. For these scientists, as the argument goes, a lockdown of society can be seen as a scientific experiment based on a liberal narrative rather than one based on a fully justified public need. Deniers also describe this in terms that can sound something like a liberal truth regime discussed earlier.

16.3 COVID-19 as a Hoax

While the deniers by and large share the kinds of concerns that skeptics raise, they take an additional step and wrap the numbers into a conspiratorial critique of contemporary political systems. They portray the numbers as part of a broader pattern of politics put forward by liberals and progressives seeking to take over society via repressive measures. Interestingly, it is a narrative that does not sound much different to the one climate deniers put forth. Indeed, the Heartland Institute and other right-wing climate deniers have themselves taken up the cause, arguing that the threats presented by COVID-19 are significantly exaggerated and are nothing much to worry about (Thies 2020).

Hardcore deniers see, often in no uncertain terms, COVID-19 measures as part of an insidious plot on the part of big government technocrats to take control and rob individuals of their basic freedoms of speech and the right to assemble. For them, this radically violates the fundamental values embedded in the conservative version of the American story. To give several slightly paraphrased examples of these harsh claims, a Pentecostal pastor and conspiracy theorist has portrayed the public health response to COVID-19 as a "phantom plague." He describes it as "part of a plot involving the Rockefeller Foundation and the World Health Organization, whose goals [are] forced vaccinations and mass murder" (Wilson 2020). Another has described the virus as "a weapon of our enemy to enslave us to fears of the virus." And yet another has argued that the virus is a hoax "being used as a completely exaggerated, super-hyped, super-inflated psychological ... campaign against the American public – a coordinated full court press of intimidation and fear-mongering by government, the mass media and the CDC" (Wilson 2020).

Employed as an opportunity to use the COVID-19 outbreak to entrench repressive measures, denialists argue that the government polices violate their constitutional rights. Stories about virus-tracing measures, for example, focus on growing surveillance of the citizenry, restrictions on free expression, the increased collection of private information (often from cell phones), the tracing of people's movements, crackdowns on dissent, imposition of curfews, limitations on public gatherings, censorship of the news media, harassment of journalists and the use of the military to police the streets. Although others see many of these as temporary measures in the face of the health crisis, hardcore deniers portray them as part of a deliberate design to restrict basic freedoms that will not necessarily be reinstated. Taken as a whole, these denier narratives offer arguments of creeping authoritarian politics.

It is notable that this latter concern is shared by many on both the political right and the left, though it is most common on the political right. For the left, the narrative is interpreted as a story about fascism raising its head; for the right it is socialism on the march. People on the left point to the worrisome rise of authoritarian measures around the world, not only in newer, weak democracies such as Hungary and Thailand, but also in stronger, traditional democracies such as the United States and Britain (Gebrekidan 2020). In the case of the radical deniers on the right, as one observer has put it, "right-wing groups . . . believe everything is a conspiracy by government [and that] big government is trying to intrude into our lives" (cited in Slessor 2020). In this story, governments are "illegitimately trying to close down business, put people out of work [and] control how close people can stand to each other" (Slessor 2020).

Important also are extreme right-wing political party leaders who see COVID-19 denial as a way to increase their political profile, the Alternative for Germany party being a good case in point. As the party was losing political stature with the public, its leaders attempted to regain their status by spreading narratives that questioned the public health measures introduced by Chancellor Merkel's government, both wearing masks and the sheltering-in-place "lockdown."[13] Here again, the pandemic initiatives are said to constitute a "deep state" ("tief Staat") plot on the part of a bureaucracy dedicated to expanding its power. In the United States, subversive bureaucrats are similarly said to be exploiting the virus as a way to topple the Trump presidency (Sullivan 2020).

16.4 Conspiracy and the Dark Web

Further, there are "dark web" conspiratorial groups that manipulate the COVID-19 information with storylines designed to sow discord and disruption via social media. Their target is the significant numbers of people in countries around the world who are, for one reason or another, highly susceptible to right-wing manipulative machinations. They appeal especially to the many who are exceedingly anxious about how they will be able to pay the rent and put food on the table. These narrative-based arguments create high degrees of distrust given the extensive economic inequalities and social anxieties that confront the susceptible. In the United States, these are manifested in stories about the wealthy 1 percent of the citizenry lining their own pockets, as well as how poor people and underserving immigrants are overburdening social welfare systems.

The discursive tactics of pandemic deniers are often quite subtle. For a common example, deniers often ask people to think about why the economy has been shut down. Who is responsible for this and why, particularly when the

---

[13] Merkel is described as the "Corona dictator." Some of them argue that the vaccination is designed to alter the DNA of those who take it.

disease can be compared to a bad case of the flu? Their narratives typically suggest plots that indict a hidden political establishment and the nefarious media it controls (Warzel 2020). QAnon describes a conspiracy on the part of Satan-worshiping deep state elites who seek to destroy Trump and the country. As a right-wing Breitbart journalist tells it, the liberal establishment "media's blatant lies are only adding to this uncertainty and fear – and are doing it by design" (Nolte 2020). For them, COVID-19 is presented as nothing more than a liberal-media-hyped "hoax."

Some conspiracy theorists argue that COVID-19 is a bioweapon developed in a Chinese laboratory. Others believe that the new 5G high-speed wireless technology network introduced by China is responsible for the spread of the virus. This narrative aligns with Trump's attempt to blame China with racist rhetoric, referring to the "Kung Flu."

Other narrative-based arguments assert that the virus was created and unleashed by the billionaire Bill Gates to permit his foundation to exert control over the world economy. Gates is in some ways an easy target for this rhetoric, as he emerged as a leading establishment spokesperson and funder of efforts to find a vaccine for the virus. As argued in this conspiracy narrative, the plan is to use the vaccine to take over and control the global economy for the purpose of making huge profits. There is often an anti-Semitic ring to such narrative accusations (Laitman 2020).

These virus denial narratives have gained traction in the United States, Britain and elsewhere. In the USA and Britain, this has to do with the fact that the President and Prime Minister, though to a lesser degree, have thwarted efforts to contain the spread of the disease. Both have stoked "cultural wars" with the help of the right-wing media in their respective countries. In many cases, these provocations have played on the prejudices of bigots, racists and xenophobes. Among them, according to Carol Johnson, are people who believe that the virus was sent "by God as a punishment for support of same-sex rights and for challenging traditional gender roles between men and women" (cited in Slessor 2020).

Prime Minister Johnson often failed to enforce social distancing practices, stressing the importance of individual freedoms (John 2020). The situation is even more dramatic in the United States. Trump argued that the threat is overblown and called on his political supporters to "liberate" states governed by Democrats from shelter-in-place rules designed to stem the circulation of the virus. Trump's message led to demonstrations in numerous states across the country, at times featuring guns in state legislatures, as well as death threats to medical doctors and other health professionals (Martelle 2020). To underscore this, Trump has generally refused to wear a face mask in an apparent effort to underplay the seriousness of the situation. He has argued that Biden supporters wear masks as a sign of political opposition. And not without success: As one Trump supporter put it, "It's all fake. They are making the numbers up. I haven't seen anybody die, not from coronavirus. I don't even know anybody who's got it." Another argued that "If it is God's will that I get coronavirus that is the will of the Almighty. I will not live in fear" (quoted in Shear, Haberman and Herdon 2020).

In this discussion of narratives and their related arguments put forward by climate change and COVID-19 deniers we have seen that it is not the numbers per se, but rather their implications for societal goals and values that drives their concerns. In the next section, we examine more specifically how these narratives about societal goals and values fit into the policy denial arguments. However, before doing this, it is important to acknowledge that it isn't easy to capture the dynamics of such argumentation, as it can move in various directions, sometimes unpredictably, depending in part on the discursive creativity of the participants. What we can do, however, is present something of an ideal type that offers a general illustration of the process, particularly the way policy measures relate to higher-level goals and values. It can, at a minimum, show policy analysts what to expect, what to look for and how to respond.

17 Narrative Arguments and the Policy-Analytic Challenge: Interpreting COVID-19 Statistics in Social Context

The key concern, as we have indicated along the way, is how people can deny COVID-19 in the face of the empirical facts presented by leading health scientists around the world. How can the policy analyst respond to such denial? Is there a discursive logic to such policy argumentation that can inform a meaningful and effective response to the deniers? In what follows, we propose a role for the policy investigator as analytic interpreter of how the issues are constructed and what they mean in the public deliberative processes.

Basic to the approach is attention to policy narratives and the arguments embedded in them – that is, arguments that are either implicit or explicit in the narratives (Roe 2020; Miller 2020), or what can be called "narrative arguments." In what follows, we focus on the arguments and understand the narratives to be their foundations, as sources of both beliefs and of evidence for those beliefs. We employ an interpretive logic of practical argumentation to tease out the arguments in, or related to, the denial narratives.

The concept of narrative argument captures the interaction of two different modes of knowing (Gubrium and Holstein 2009). The narrative mode of knowing is an account of a sequences of events, usually (but not always) structured around a beginning, a middle and an end, as in a literary story. The argumentative dimension is generally organized around premises and a conclusion, which can be analytically approached with an informal, abductive logic of practical inference. Taken as a whole, a narrative argument is a dynamic interpretive mode of inference that emerges through interactive processes among arguers and audience (Al Tamimi 2016). The narrative component can emerge in discussions as replies to statements or arguments, and can include emotional and motivational components designed to persuade. Given that the elements of narrative arguments interact in complex ways, it can be difficult to analytically separate the parts without risking some loss of attention to their persuasive force. The interpretive process of narrative argument, in this regard, cannot be simply reduced to premises and conclusions; to capture the full force of the argument and its various features – procedural, inferential, emotional and substantive – there needs to be an ongoing recognition of the interactive discursive connections among the component parts.

The goal of such analysis is to identify the critical points of political controversy and the way that meaningful deliberations might be facilitated. This can be pursued by drawing on the abductive methods[14] of interpretive policy analysis to examine the narrative construction of the COVID-19 denial arguments (Yanow 2000). Focusing on the discursive politics of post-truth, we employ a four-level interpretive framework to draw out the ways the argumentative elements carried by the narratives are put forward by Covid denialists. Outlining the structure of the policy arguments and the ways they can be interpreted by the participants, the task of this abductive inferential logic is to more closely identify, explicate and interpret the key empirical and normative elements and the agreements and disagreements to which they give rise.

17.1 Levels of COVID-19 Policy Argumentation

Turning to the levels of policy argument, we draw on the logic of practical reason, adapted to policy argumentation (Fischer 1995). Beginning with the first-order assessment of COVID-19 arguments, the focus is on a technical-empirical evaluation of a program outcome (does the program work?), followed by an interpretation of how the program relates to the context to which it applies (i.e., is it relevant to the situation?). It then shifts to a higher, second-order assessment that examines the program's consequences for the larger social system of which it is a part, followed by an interpretive explication of the

---

[14] Abduction, as a mode of inference, refers to a constructive form of reasoning that seeks a plausible conclusion, though not formally verified with deductive logic. It pursues the best possible argument to interpret and explain a phenomenon or event from the information available.

value implications (reflected in the dominant ideologies) pertinent to a final policy judgment (Fischer 1995).[15]

Although the argumentation often starts at the ideological level in political struggles, especially in the case of politicians, we begin with the more concrete level, as this is typically where policy analysts enter the argumentative process; this offers the advantage of first speaking directly to the kinds of arguments most often put to policy analysts. Here, the emphasis is on a policy program. The question is, in ordinary language, does it work? It is a question that is typically addressed empirically using the technical criteria of efficiency or effectiveness.

Drawing primarily on the COVID-19 case in the United States, supported with illustrations from Britain, Germany and Thailand, we can begin with the most concrete arguments embedded in the narratives – namely, the empirical claims and their situational implications. As we shall see, it also addresses a primary concern put forward by COVID-19 denial narratives. By setting the technical-analytic arguments in their interpretive context, it becomes possible to give more nuanced and meaningful answers to the deniers than just emphasizing the technical data.

17.2 Program Outcomes and the Interpretation of the COVID-19 Statistics

No policy question at the techno-empirical level is more important than those that pertain to the shelter-in-place policy – or the so-called "lockdown" – that was ordered across countries such as the United States, Britain, Germany and Thailand, among many others. This lockdown was primarily decided on the basis of statistical data indicating the rate of infections across the society, with special attention to their implications for the capacities of hospitals in particular locations to deal with those who contracted the disease. A main policy question, then, concerns the degree to which the general lockdown has been successful in reducing the rate of infections. Basic to this question are issues about the verification of the medical statistics used as the basis for mandating the lockdown policy, where and how the numbers were collected, as well as questions about when to end the lockdown. For many of the deniers, as we have noted, the medical statistics alone did not justify the lockdowns. They argue that the resulting measures were presented as if all situational contexts were equal – region, age, health conditions, etc. – without noting that circumstances vary from context to context and that one rule does not fit all.

---

[15] Both first- and second-order assessments and their interrelated components are all part of a complete practical argument.

An interpretive policy analyst can introduce here the constructivist understanding of statistics. From this perspective, it is possible to understand how some of the denier's objections can be valid without necessarily leading to a rejection of lockdown measures. To introduce this perspective, one can usefully recall Mark Twain's famous quip about "lies, damned lies and statistics," a phase frequently invoked by people who object to particular statistical outcomes. It has, in fact, long been recognized that statistics are not necessarily what they purport to be. Statisticians, according to this understanding, do not necessarily utter things they know to be false; rather, it is more a matter of where they put the emphasis in their interpretations of the numbers (Porter 1995).

The interpretive analyst can approach this by explaining that statistics are best understood by acknowledging the social dimensions involved in their construction. As Best (2012: 27) has written, "all statistics, as products of social activities, are socially constructed."

Whereas people often see statistics as measures of truth, they can better be seen as precious stones that need to be selected, cut with precision, carefully polished and situated in settings that permit them to be observed from different angles (Best 2012). The analyst's interpretive task here is to explain to those denying the statistics that it is a matter concerned with a mix of both social construction and empirical calculation.

17.3 COVID-19 Policy Statistics in Narrative Arguments

At this juncture, a policy analyst can introduce the COVID-19 deniers to the constructivist interpretation of knowledge and expertise, in particular to the way it applies to statistics. Fundamental to a constructivist analysis, it will be recalled, is the role of social context, as the setting that supplies the perspectives of interpretation. Insofar as the deniers argue that the experts are socially biased, this provides an opportunity to offer a better understanding of how science and expertise works without forfeiting or denying the social element. Fundamental here is a need for the analyst to help people understand what statistics are and what they can and cannot do. It essentially involves introducing a higher level of "statistical illiteracy."

Part of the problem, it can be explained, has to do with the very nature of statistics, especially their role in narrative-oriented argumentation. Often slighted in public narratives, including media presentations, is the well-established fact that statistical information only refers to probabilities, not to absolute certainties. Once the numbers are placed in narrative contexts, however, they tend to take on lives of their own in different settings. After the statistics are introduced, they often focus public debate in ways that imply they mean more than they do.

In the case of COVID-19 statistics, the numbers offer essential information but do not constitute a complete picture, as good statisticians will themselves point out. Moreover, the interpretation of the probabilities will often be influenced by the ideological orientation of the interpreter and the particular situational context to which the statistics refer, the context itself being a social construction. These percentages, then, provide opportunities for people – whatever their ideological bent – to raise questions and argue about how to interpret them and what they mean in different contexts. They thus open the door for those intent on manipulating the interpretations for questionable reasons. By wrapping the numbers into particular stories related to different social contexts, actors can significantly, sometimes dramatically, alter their meanings in policy arguments. It is important, then, for the policy analyst to better illustrate the contextually oriented social processes involved in the construction and narrative presentation of the statistics and be prepared to explain them to the consumers of these numbers, the deniers in particular. A good statistician, it can be pointed out, will concede that the construction of statistics depends on numerous factors, starting with which question is asked. Who selected the variables to be measured, and for which reason? Why were the statistical categories constructed in a particular way? How were the groups narratively defined? Which elements were excluded and why (Schield 2007)?

On a more fundamental level, the interpretive analyst needs to explain that numbers in policy processes are reflections of social and political activities. As Stone (1988:137) has put it, all parties to a deliberation have to recognize that numbers in politics "are measurements of human activities, made by human beings, and intended to influence human behavior." They are, as such, "subject to conscious and unconscious manipulation by the people being measured, the people making the measurements, and the people who interpret and use measures made by others."

In her seminal work on public policy storytelling and the role of numbers, Stone has further shown how counting, including statistical counting, can function interpretively like a social metaphor. This can occur as the interpretive process of narratively defining the contextual boundaries of the empirical categories serves to create social or political communities. As she writes, "any number is implicitly an assertion that things counted in it share a common feature and should be treated as a group, either natural or statistical . . . in order to demonstrate common interests or concerns and thereby stimulate creation of a natural community," a group of citizens infected with COVID-19 being a case in point. In this way, counting can also be used for social and political mobilization (Stone 1988: 136). The medical statistics related to COVID-19, for example, have been narrated in ways aimed to mobilize political decisions to shut down societies around the world. To establish and narrate common or shared problems, or characteristics among individuals with and without COVID-19 is, then, to interpretively place them into contextual groups, however artificial the classification might be.

Numerical measurement can, as such, interpretively supply a normative storyline with an implicit call for action, as was the case for mask wearing and the politics of lockdown. We see this in both the case of the government's argument for mitigating action and the political behavior of those who oppose the measures. It shows how we count things when we seek to change them, or to alter the behavior of others in a situation, such as sheltering-at-home or wearing protective face masks. Not only can presenting the measurement of a problem in a particular way establish a subtle pressure to change it, as Stone (1988:131) puts it, "some level of measure usually becomes established as a norm" in narrative explanations of government policies. And it is the establishment of such norms – which can turn into hard facts rather than interpretative assessments – related to COVID-19 that worries the critics of statistics on both the political right and the left. For them, the statistics are chosen as part of a narrative argument devoted to justifying greater control of the public, especially over the long-run as established norms can be difficult to remove.

Moreover, the norms that result from statistical measures are sometimes contextually ambiguous, especially when they are simultaneously interpreted by competing storytellers. In Great Britain, for example, Prime Minister Johnson was accused of promulgating confusing, ambiguous norms pertaining to the return to work – not only being heavily criticized by his political opponents, but also providing fodder for the comic storylines of British comedians.

17.4 COVID-19 Statistics as Political Strategy

Statistics are especially prominent in stories about crisis, related to both decline and the need for political action (Stone 1988: 134). Such storylines are found in the COVID-19 denial arguments, particularly as they portend economic decline if drastic action is not taken. Equally important here is the way a story based on numbers can carry a hidden or implicit message. The act of counting itself can function as an implicit argument indicating that when an event happens often enough to justify being counted, it tends to become assumed to be politically meaningful and taken seriously (Stone 2020). Measurement, in this way, has to be recognized as part of a sociopolitical process interpreted in particular contexts.

Thus, COVID-19 numbers in policy arguments cannot be adequately comprehended without interpretively examining how they are assembled, calculated and told. Why are some items counted and not others? In what way is the connection between the measurements and the items measured determined? Are there strategic political incentives to interpret some numbers as being higher or lower (Stone 1988)? In seeking to change activities, people attempt to influence those who do the measuring and interpret their meanings. Trump's narrative struggles with both the leaders of the CDC and the WHO are cases in point. In his story, as noted earlier, the high COVID-19 infection numbers are inaccurate and deliberatively used to stand in the way of his calls for returning to economic activity. He does this by narrating an alternative interpretation of the WHO and what it is purported to be up to. Trump's argument was widely seen as an effort to change the organization's counting practices in ways that would favor his COVID-19 narrative.

The selection of the context for making sense of statistics is a strategic aspect of both problem definition and policy design, particularly as the findings of the measures assume a political dimension in the competing interpretations. This, in fact, is just what the critics of the lockdown argue. It is the underlying Covid stories into which the numbers are contextually situated that serve as the foundation of an interpretation of the problem. For example, the issuance of health passports to some citizens who have tested negatively for COVID-19 and not to others who tested positive not only puts them into different social categories, but situationally brands them respectively with particular narratives as "desirable" and "undesirable" people.

The point here for policy analysis is the need to step out of a strictly empirical orientation and interpretively discuss statistics in terms of their relationship to their context. This not only contributes to a more honest form of policy deliberation, but also offers an approach that deals with the sorts of issues raised by the skeptics and the deniers. Insofar as they are convinced that there are social considerations influencing or biasing the COVID-19 statistics, such deliberative argumentation offers an opportunity to explain the ways in which they are not altogether wrong, while also showing that this concession does not mean the statistics are of no value. And, in doing so, it can help to undercut an important social dynamic at play here – namely, that when the deniers feel slighted or ignored by the media or the experts, they tend become more convinced that something is not right and conclude that their point of view is not being heard.

When this social aspect of statistics is openly presented as an inherent part of the interpretive-analytical process, there is a better chance that it can lead to a more constructive dialogue about the narrative meanings of the numbers. The fact that there is a degree of social construction built into statistical analysis does not mean that the calculations are necessarily misleading or false, as implied by the deniers. Instead, it means that there is a need for a different kind of deliberation that brings the statistics and policy goals together with a consideration of social context and narrative understanding. Short of such a discussion, both the technical experts and the deniers retreat to their respective ideologies for their own sakes. It is a result that also plays into the hands of the deniers by anointing their argument as one of the various competing viewpoints, which in turn tends to lend a measure of credibility to it.

There will still be people who refuse to listen to or be influenced by this interpretive understanding under any circumstances. We can in part understand this stance by turning to higher levels of discursive argumentation: second-order argumentation, in the practical logic of policy deliberation. It is here that the deniers part company with the mere skeptics.

18 Rejecting COVID-19 Lockdown: Interpreting Political-Economic and Ideological Arguments

A basic reason why empirical evidence does not influence hardcore deniers has to do with the fact that they are focused on defending a societal system and a way of life rather than on accepting particular statistics. This will strike many as absurd, but, as we saw in the earlier discussion of practical reason, different participants will emphasize different aspects of the overall interpretive-analytic assessment. Whereas some will see the basic problem as being located at the technical level of argumentation, others will believe it to be a problem related more significantly to the larger societal level and the interpretation of its values.

From this logic of policy argumentation, we can recognize that the accept-ability of any narrative claim ultimately depends on its relationship to a conception of the core beliefs that spell out a conception of the good society. We don't usually think this way, as in normal times the good society is taken for granted; this level of argument, as such, does not come into play. But the coronavirus pandemic is not a normal time, and its implications bring forth questions about the societal way of life itself. Aristotle (1991), perhaps the original philosopher of practical reason, helps us to interpret this would-be disconnect between mundane statistics and a way of life. For him, the validity of any statement depends on its ultimate relationship to the good – in this case, the good society.

For COVID-19 deniers, as well as climate change deniers, the fundamental concern is the defense of a free society, understood as one in which the individual is free to pursue his or her interests in both the economic and political spheres. Anything that threatens their commitment to this fundamental ideological value will be judged as problematic. Thus, beyond issues related to the correctness of the statistics, the discussion turns to questions about the implications of the policy measures for the societal system as a whole. This involves, first, a second-order assessment of the empirical consequences for the existing system and its underlying normative orientations; and, second, an interpretive-analytic assessment of the actual system's relationship to an ideal societal system.

18.1 COVID-19 and the Political-Economic System

Beginning with the existing societal system, there are two basic questions that COVID-19 deniers raise at this level of interpretive argumentation. One concerns the impact of the pandemic-response measures on the economy as a whole. Here, they express concerns about the effects of lockdown (or sheltering-in-place) on the workings of the larger political-economic system. Although this shifts the discussion toward more normative concerns, the question also involves complicated empirical issues. The emphasis for the deniers is first on concerns about the empirical impacts of the lockdown on an economic recovery. And, second, the deniers want to know who is responsible for making these political and economic decisions and why?

The COVID-19 deniers' concerns about the impact of the lockdown pose difficult questions, about which experts, politicians and citizens can disagree, taking the interpretive task into uncharted territories. There has never been such a major shut down of the economic system. Everybody recognizes that the virus has thrown the economies of the world into recession – if not depression, in some cases. Moreover, we do not yet know the full impact of the lockdown, making it difficult to interpretively assess the consequences. But what the deniers can and do argue, with some justification, is that there was not enough attention to these concerns at the outset.

For one thing, deniers argue that the costs of the cure could end up being worse than the damage caused by the disease itself. As economies dramatically shrink, many of the goods and services upon which contemporary life depends will not be available. People without work, they argue, will not have the money to purchase food, medical supplies and other necessities. In some parts of the world, people will die of hunger because of the virus. Such shortages will lead to increased levels of civil disruption, and even violence. It is further pointed out that the lockdown will lead to a range of psychological problems, some of which can arise from loneliness and others from domestic stress. In addition, other non-Covid illnesses which can also lead to death will go unattended. To be sure, the COVID-19 measures involve heavy economic costs that need to be compared with the human health costs.

For this reason, the deniers interpret lockdown as too restrictive and call for a relatively quick reopening of the economy. They also contend that a lockdown's ancillary measures, such as the wearing of protective masks and following the rules of social distancing, do not facilitate the reopening of the economic system. But, in so arguing, they tend to largely ignore the fact that further lockdowns resulting from the failure to wear masks will be even more damaging to the economy.

Beyond the lay interpretations of deniers, the attempt to vindicate a policy goal such as societal lockdown has its academic counterpart. Formal political-economic analysis can, as such, inform this discussion. Methodologically, this involves an effort to rigorously examine the empirical and normative consequences for system-wide performance. Specifically, does the policy goal instrumentally facilitate the institutional practices, norms and values of the larger political-economic system? As one policy scholar has put it, the analysts must at this point replace "their methodological microscope with a theoretical macroscope" so that they can "concentrate on the relationship between public policy and the overall political-economic system" (deHaven Smith 1988: 49).

Given the nature of the questions at this level of policy argumentation, the full vindication of a policy goal for the system as a whole generally requires the passage of time. While the more immediate benefits of a program to participants can usually be established within a reasonable period of time, it takes much longer for the consequences of the policy goals to manifest themselves in the larger societal system, including the inevitable unexpected consequences. This uncertainty and disagreement leaves plenty of room for interpretive politics.

The assessment is further complicated by the fact that we are in a situation for which there are no parallel experiences from which to draw. There are good chances that the economic system will never return to the "old normal." It may well involve a massive restructuring that is beyond our ability to estimate, affecting all areas of modern society – education, transportation, food supply, shopping, climate change, hotels and tourism, modes of social interaction, public security and more.

As an interpretive-analytical test of the instrumental or contributive value of the policy's goals and assumptions for the larger societal system, the inquiry requires the support of social science and its techniques. This could involve a form of systems analysis, including one of its key methods: cost–benefit analysis (Weimer and Vining 2017). The systems approach can offer a form of "macro" cost–benefit analysis (Schmid 1989). While this involves a much more difficult empirical analysis, requiring a wider range of system-related costs and benefits, the basic logic of the method is largely the same.

18.2 Whose Interpretation Governs the System?

Part of the meaning of such an assessment for deniers will depend on the second question that lurks behind the empirical and methodological issues – namely, who is interpreting the political-economic system, and how does it work? The conservative narrative of the deniers typically assumes a free enterprise system based on the individual, with the individual entrepreneur taken to be the driving force. The deniers will thus judge the statistical numbers in terms of their implications for the market system and its primary actors. But a key question that divides the competing groups relates to alternative interpretations of the American system more generally. This is part of a long-standing debate regarding the extent to which a particular understanding of the system actually conforms to reality? The system, in short, is so complex that the question does not lend itself to definitive interpretation. For example, free-market ideology aside, the political-economic system is in reality dominated by big corporations and a large governmental system, both with massive power over small entrepreneurs. Whereas conservatives harshly criticize the bureaucratic governmental system, they continue to speak as if a corporate system represents free enterprise. They also show little concern when the government gives billions of Covid-related dollars to large corporations (at the expense of small, free-market businesses), but complain when the government seek to support the health care of workers and poor people seeking assistance in the face of the virus.

For those deniers who subscribe to conspiratorial theories, the blame for a false understanding of the system is attributed to the dominant "deep state" economic elites, Bill Gates being one of their primary targets. Acceptance of the outcomes of the decisions will thus in significant ways turn on the concepts of social justice and democracy embedded in the respective narratives. That is, the future course of the political economy will depend on more than just calculations based on existing arrangements. This question of political control over the system raises questions that shift the argumentative discourse to more fundamental ideological concerns related to the ideal societal system.

For many of the deniers, the primary concern driving their complaints is less about the specific programmatic outcomes than it is about who is responsible for them. Deniers typically identify establishment elites and deep state bureaucrats as responsible for shaping the policies that lead to the system outcomes. In their view, lockdown measures are imposed as part of a strategic attempt to take over and restructure the American political economy in the interest of establishing greater social control and accruing larger private profits. Similar to the political narrative that Hofstadter (2012) showed to be running throughout American political history, they charge elites with political manipulation of the system. In short, it is not just the outcomes but also the underlying political goals and objectives that are at issue. Conspiratorial advocates, including the COVID-19 deniers, have leaned on Trump's rhetoric promise to clean the elite "swamp" in Washington.

This perspective, in fact, rests on a long-standing political question that political scientists and sociologists have debated since the beginnings of their fields. Although they approach the question in a much more sophisticated way than the deniers, some do argue that the entire sociopolitical system is controlled by a handful of wealthy elites. Others, in disagreement, contend the system is too complex and pluralistic for any particular group to amass this kind of power. And yet others argue that it is the experts rather than the wealthy who pull the strings.

The difficulty of this assessment is that there is no way to empirically prove in any final way which theory is accurate. This has to do with the sheer complexity of the system, coupled with other factors such as the difficulties in empirically "operationalizing" the hidden and tacit manipulations of the elites. Thus, what one has to do is amass as much evidence as possible, both facts and narrative stories, and use it to interpretively judge the competing theories. But, as the history of the debates in political science and sociology have long shown, there is no way to settle this argument to the satisfaction of everyone. In the end, people can always find a reason to disagree with a particular assessment. They thus rely on their ideological beliefs in an attempt to interpret the question for themselves.

18.3 COVID-19 as a Challenge to Social and Political Values

This point brings us to the ideological level of policy argumentation. At this level, the deniers put their emphasis on concerns about freedom, liberty and a limited form of government that does not trample on their understanding of the Constitutional right to assemble. Numerous commentators have argued that the failed response to COVID-19 in the United States is lodged the country's libertarian political culture, in particular its emphasis on the individual citizen and the pursuit of self-interest. Tending to distrust government from the outset, the citizenry is often too unwilling to acknowledge a need to help fellow citizens, which is reflected in a reluctance to accept public interventions that can protect their fellow citizens in need. As Krugman (2020) has put it, he knows of "no other advanced country … that has a comparable number of people who respond with rage when asked to wear a mask in a supermarket." Or any other country "where demonstrators against public health measures would wave guns around and invade state capitols" (Krugman 2020).

In short, the ideological issues that the deniers raise are essentially questions related to political philosophy, even if not rigorously formulated. Although much of what political philosophers do is generally seen to fall outside of the purview of policy analysis, the interpretive logic of argumentation shows that this is not necessarily the case. Even though most policy issues do not raise questions of political philosophy, they sometimes do so. Indeed, a number of theorists have shown the ways that such issues can come into play in policy inquiry focused on contemporary policy problems (MacRae 1976; Anderson 1978). This was particularly visible during the "Reagan Revolution," when a resurgent conservative movement asked fundamental questions about the relation of liberal policies to the nation's fundamental values. That set in motion debates that reshaped American political discourse, extending to today's conservative deniers, related both to climate change and COVID-19.

At this ideological level, the ultimate interpretive task of practical argumentation involves an attempt to justify a choice of one way of life over another (Fischer 2003). In terms of formal political philosophy, a major task is to construct models of the good way of life by identifying the importance of a particular political value or values (such as freedom, equality or community) that should be taken as the ultimate goal(s) of all political undertakings. Each political theorist attempts to make a case for one set of social and political values over another. Thus, for example, some will argue that freedom is the highest value for a society to strive for, whereas others will disagree, contending that social welfare should carry as much or more weight as freedom.

The task is to interpretively assess what will occur if a societal system emphasizes a particular value or set of values as opposed to others. The question is not unlike the one asked in the attempt to justify or reject the implications for the political-economic system; the difference is that it's applied to an ideal sociopolitical system as opposed to an existing regime. Empirical information can be brought to the analysis, but it can only be a component of a larger interpretive inquiry that also includes speculation and imagination. Through the speculative creation of alternative political systems, the political theorist seeks to imagine and illustrate the consequences resulting from prioritizing a particular value and/or the implications of the neglect of another value (Rawls 1971). Existing evidence related to the instrumental implications, short of proof, can be garnered to support the construction of one vision over another. In policy analysis, Grauhan and Strubelt (1971) employ this political logic to make a case for emphasizing the principle of self-realization, somewhat similar to Sen's (1993) argument about human social capacities.

It is this question that deniers raise, though in less rigorous everyday terms. Essentially, they interpret freedom to be a higher value than others such as social welfare, community or human health. With regard to COVID-19, deniers contend that people have the right to decide freely how they will respond to the dangers posed by the virus. Some of them will choose more risk than others, independently of what government experts advise. They also maintain that people should be free to go back to work. If the economy sinks too low under lockdown, they argue, people will begin to suffer from other problems that can be as dangerous as the virus, hunger in particular. Without work people will be unable to buy food or pay the rent. They should thus be free to return to their jobs.

The neglect of freedom as the organizing principle of society, in this view, leads to a type of society in which they wish not to live. For many deniers, the government's COVID-19 measures are authoritarian and bring socialist government, sooner if not later. For many of them, as we saw, the measures are even seen as a deliberate strategy to impose socialism. Some portray it as a question of "do or die."

But what they ignore, as others point out, is that no one value stands entirely alone. All values in a functioning society are part of a value system. The relationships of the different values in a given society are generally understood by its citizens and leaders, even if imperfectly. A society can emphasize a particular value, but this does not mean that the other values simply disappear or that they do not need attention. Freedom, for example, also generally implies social responsibility.

The neglect of social responsibility is reflected in the deniers' failures to recognize or concede that their dominant emphasis on freedom at any cost endangers their fellow citizens. They fail, in short, to acknowledge that a singular focus on one value in all circumstances can lead to problems that will not only affect others, but will also return to limit their own freedoms. In the case at hand, the irresponsible exercise of freedom can contribute not only to a denial of their fellow citizens' right to a healthy environment, but also to a dramatic spread of the virus that can prolong the reopening of the economy. As leading medical experts have argued, in this case wearing a mask can actually lead the way to greater freedom. Rather than having to shelter at home, people would be able return to a more normal life outside, and even go to work in the office.

We can also see here a form of countersystems analysis at work. It was for some time customary for the COVID-19 deniers to point to Sweden as the countermodel, as that country had decided not to enforce lockdown. The Swedish model depended on voluntary measures on the part of the citizens. Citizens, it was argued, would do the right thing. But before long Sweden was experiencing rates of Covid infection worse than their neighboring countries of Denmark and Finland, both of which had introduced strict lockdown measures. We have since learned that many factors contributed to this outcome – with various contextual unknowns – which makes it difficult to adapt the Swedish experience to other countries.

Finally, what the deniers have also failed to recognize, particularly in the context of policy argumentation, is that all rules and laws typically carry their own exceptions. Already, we have seen that the logic of policy argumentation allows for exceptions to a particular rule if it is interpreted to be inappropriate to a particular social context. This can mean that while freedom is the highest value, it has to be exempted in the situational context of COVID-19 and that such a decision is in the interest of all.[16]

19 Deliberating with Post-Truth Deniers: Concluding Remarks

Finally, we come to a concluding discussion. Here we can bring together essential points from the foregoing text to offer several insights to guide policy analysts in engaging with the climate and COVID-19 deniers. Before doing that, however, it is important to underscore two basic points. The first is the recognition that we are dealing with a political issue. Post-truth cannot, as such, be resolved simply by recourse to better information and the facilitation of deliberative argumentation. At the same time, though, given that argumentation is part of political struggle, there is a role here for public reason and political deliberation, a process which policy analysts can help to promote (Jasanoff and Simmet 2017).

Second, we need to again emphasize the need for science and expertise. Putting aside the thorny and complex philosophical issues involved in defining "truth," scientific findings are essential for dealing successfully with both climate change and COVID-19. Having said that, however, it is important to reiterate that science alone cannot solve the climate change or COVID-19 denial problems. The denial of both, as we have stressed all along, is essentially a political problem and has to be confronted as such.

Regarding deliberation, the interpretive policy analyst can offer perspectives that help to improve the quality of argumentation in policy discourse. Of particular importance, as we have seen, is the interpretive analyst's ability to respond to these controversies by getting past the standard attempts to reinforce the emphasis on empirical evidence. In this regard, an interpretive approach can

---

[16] In law, there is a practical example that illustrates this point: You are allowed to shout "fire," but not in a crowded theater. The exception is introduced to avoid dangerous consequences of stampeding.

enter into the discursive context and examine how the evidence is constructed and fitted into the sociopolitical narratives that undergird denial arguments. By interpretively teasing out the ways such competing narratives and arguments give the empirical-analytic information social and political meaning, analysts can contribute to a better understanding of how to deliberate post-truth conflicts with deniers.

Part of the problem with the traditional empirical modes of policy analysis has been the inability of its practitioners to include and interpret social meanings on their own terms. This, as we discussed at the outset, is a result of the practices associated with the positivist conception of knowledge, namely ruling out attention to the subjective dimensions of human behavior. By emphasizing the observable dimensions of a social phenomenon, the positivist/empiricist sees the world through a different lens than do their subjects. Their models tend to be constructed around the investigator's implicit, tacit assumptions and value judgments about the phenomenon in question. They thus neglect a careful consideration of the social context by imposing assumptions on the situation; unwittingly, they are prone to substituting their own views of the social situation for those of the actors. The interpretive policy approach seeks to bring the actors themselves back into the analysis.

19.1 Learning to Listen and Acknowledge

The importance of this methodological limitation is illustrated in an interview with Oreskes (see Chotiner 2020) about how to speak to deniers. She has pointed to the need to understand and acknowledge the deniers' own ways of thinking. Recognizing that the psychology of denial is more complex than generally assumed, Oreskes begins with the obvious point: people are not happy to receive bad news. Most people do not particularly like accepting ideas that clash with their beliefs or with how they wish to live their own lives. In the case of COVID-19, they are used to going out to visit families and friends, have drinks in bars and so on. But the virus, they are suddenly told, means that all of this has to be put on hold, if not come to an end altogether. This means, Oreskes argues, that these people should first hear that their concerns are understood. The experts have to be willing to concede to the deniers that their resistance is understandable, even reasonable, under particular circumstances.[17] In short, it is a miserable situation

---

[17] "Nobody wants to be stuck in their house for the next six months, or possibly longer. Most people like to go out to restaurants, bars, clubs. We like to go to our gym. We like to go to work. We like to not be laid off" (Chotiner 2020: x).

that needs to be honestly recognized, as a mark of validation of their feelings.

Acknowledging these feelings can help to establish a connection capable of creating a degree of trust that might facilitate a discussion with the deniers. This, then, could become the basis for the more difficult task of explaining that denial will not make this unpleasant reality go away and that we can only come to grips with it collectively. The goal here is to establish a foundation for a collaborative interaction. Such interaction requires a deliberative process based on both reasoned argumentation and authentic intersubjective communication.

There are, however, numerous reasons why such narrative deliberation is impeded. With the assistance of a large literature on deliberative processes, ranging from theoretical work on deliberative democracy to the interpretive practices of deliberative policy analysis, policy experts can better understand such blockages (Bächtiger et al. 2018). These approaches are designed to find ways to bring experts and citizens together in a deliberation of relevant narrative-based facts, meanings and values that illustrates what different discursive constructions would mean for policy decisions pertaining to specific situations (Fischer 2003: 221–237; Hajer and Wagenaar 2003; Fischer and Boossabong 2018). Grounded in the "argumentative turn," the effort to better grasp this coproduction of knowledge and understandings is central to the interpretive practices of deliberative policy analysis.

19.2 Toward an Integrated Framework

Such deliberation needs to be guided by an integrated framework of empirical and interpretive inquiry. The development of such a methodological framework has been a primary mission of deliberative policy analysis. The goal of the framework employed here is to include technical data, but to interpret it in the contexts – local, societal and ideological – in which the policies are embedded (Fischer 2003; 2009). Toward this end, the assignment is to enable a dialectical exchange between the theoretical knowledge of the expert and the ordinary knowledge of policymakers and citizens (whatever their differing points of view), including lay knowledge pertinent to the specific decisions at hand (Fischer 2009). The challenge has led to an emphasis on participatory collaboration in policy inquiry (Healy 1997).

This does not render science less important, as some tend to fear. But it does mean that scientific judgments have to be understood as important factors for consideration rather than as definitive answers. Those engaged in decision-making processes always need to weigh the technical findings against various social and pragmatic considerations. Such judgments require a multi-disciplinary interpretive perspective. Under such circumstances, policy decisions are best taken after deliberating the issues from competing points of view, both scientific and normative (Fischer 2009). It is necessary, in short, to consider the competing views that can legitimately evaluate and judge the normative implications of the various decision options and interpret them against the values and goals of the particular communities. For this reason, scientific and technical bodies are not the only groups capable of proffering valid opinions about a particular situation. Others with different modes of reason can also make important interpretations related to the same phenomena (Stillitoe 2007: 1–22). At specific points, as the sociology of science has demonstrated, this also includes citizens with relevant experiences (Fischer 2000). Not only do lay citizens often have access to particular facts of the situation needed by the decision-makers confronted with climate change and COVID-19, the political legitimacy they can supply is often important for the effective implementation of policies (Fischer 2009).

This is where an appreciation of the policy perspective becomes especially important. Policymaking in a democratic society is about more than science and expertise. Policy is inevitably an amalgam of expert, political and citizen knowledge, interpretive judgments and opinion. It emerges from a larger consideration that includes what we know, what has happened before, what the mediating circumstances are, what will be politically accepted and thus implementable, who benefits directly and indirectly, and more.

Politicians who have argued that they will only listen to the scientists in making COVID-19 policy decisions make a mistake here (Stephens 2020). Not only do they play into the hands of the deniers, they misinterpret the nature and formulation of public policy. Sometimes, as in the case of COVID-19, policy decisions have to be made based on the best available evidence and the exigencies of the problem to be addressed. In this sense, it can be quite appropriate at a particular time for decision-makers to act on findings that are less than desirable in an effort to reduce the risk of a disaster that could result from not acting at all. At other times, it might be necessary for policymakers to override the best available evidence. It is a matter for political judgment based on careful deliberation of the evidence, the circumstances and the normative implications of any decision. There is no escape here from the political; even the best judgment in the policy realm remains political. Ultimately, the power to decide plays a decisive role.

We can see, in short, that facts are only one component – albeit an essential component – of a larger deliberation. In this regard, we can understand Schuman's contention that the statistics can be accurate, but the judgment wrong. In the case of COVID-19, it means that questionable statistics do not necessarily mean that the lockdown measures are wrong. This underscores the importance of the interpretive policy analyst's understanding of the need to bring a wider range of social and contextual circumstances into consideration. As the constructive logic of interpretative policy argumentation helped us see, a full assessment of a measure requires using a mix of both empirical and normative criteria. An adequate judgment, as such, necessitates examining together the various components of narrative-based arguments – that is, technical, situational, systemic and ideological – to arrive at a more comprehensive understanding of what rationality means in the social world.

As far as deliberation is concerned, there is no shortage of counterpoints for the policy experts to introduce in a discussion with deniers. Especially important in this case is the fact that the experts can acknowledge the validity of specific narrative elements of denial arguments. For example, regarding the questions about statistical measures – related to either climate change or COVID-19 – it is possible to agree with the deniers that the statistics in some cases can be called into question and explain the ways social constructions of those so-called "facts" are interpreted. In this regard, analysts can show that the statistics need not be deceptively designed; rather, elements of uncertainty – both empirical and social – are inherent to the nature of the knowledge. This opens up concrete ways to discuss and assess concerns about the numbers rather than just ignoring them or writing them off as ignorant.

19.3 Speaking to the Objections

With regard to narratives about the impact of the lockdown on the economy, experts can easily concede to the deniers that the issues pose daunting questions that are full of empirical uncertainties. Basic to the narrative questions are genuine value conflicts between essential economic priorities and medical issues related to life and death. Indeed, such conflicts raise questions that can be interpreted from different perspectives. In particular, there is the question of how an economy can be reopened if starting up again causes the virus to spread to a point of economic breakdown. And there is also the question of the impact of a second wave. Would that not leave the economy in even worse shape? A workable answer to this question can only be forged through a careful collaborative deliberation involving all concerned.

The question of freedom is in some ways easier to address. Most can agree on the importance of freedom. But it should also be pointed out that the story of freedom can be told in ways that have different meanings. What is freedom about? How should it be exercised? Should there be limits on freedom under specific circumstances? Freedom cannot be interpreted to mean that people can do whatever they want all of the time. If this were the case, the system as a whole would buckle. Careful engagement with these kinds of questions might be seen as potentially offering a "metanarrative argument" (Roe 1994) that could possibly bring the groups together.

Elsewhere, I have argued that one possible bridge between the tribes of the right and those of the left could center around a discussion of their common concerns about the rise of authoritarianism and its implications for the future of democracy, particularly the sort of eco-authoritarianism that the climate crisis may well usher in (Fischer 2017). This could constitute, at least in theory, a set of concerns that might establish a basis for a discursive engagement between the deniers and the believers. Since there are some on both the right and on the left who are concerned that liberty and freedom will be threatened by more authoritarian forces, the understanding and ramifications of authoritarianism could promote a debate over their disagreements about the threat, its underlying causes and the responses to it. In the case of the deniers, it might be discovered that their expressed concerns for liberty are only a narrative cover for preserving their own economic advantages in society. Perhaps at this juncture, they would be less inclined to further engage in the debate. But making explicit their assumptions – bringing them to public attention – would be an important step toward a better understanding of the nature of the conflict (Fischer 2020).

Critical to these questions has to be the fact that for freedom to work, there have to be rules that need to be followed, particularly as they relate to social responsibilities. In this way, there are always exceptions to rules that need to be acknowledged, usually related to circumstances. When people are ill, for example, others are expected to respect the health problems of the afflicted. But it is here that trust again raises its head. It is difficult to have such a conversation about freedom and its rules with people who interpret the COVID-19 lockdown measures as a strategy to control them through restrictions on their freedom of assembly, a basic component of democratic culture.

19.4 Deliberation and Policy Learning

In the larger perspective of deliberative democracy, this should not be interpreted to mean political advocacy for particular positions. Rather than advancing particular social or political judgments (just what experts are accused of by post-truthers), policy experts can take a stance initially proposed by Dewey (1927) and devote their activities to interpreting the implications of competing positions, both empirical and normative (Fischer 2009). In this way, the policy experts become facilitators of dialogue, which can take place at every level of society, from mini-publics to society-wide forums, such as the national policy inquiries in Brazil (Pogrebinschi and Samuels 2014).

The goal of such deliberation should be "policy learning" rather than decision-making per se. Although it can make the interpretive-analytical assignment more manageable, learning is discovered not to be straightforward. People tend to resist learning that conflicts with their established beliefs. Critical learning theory, in fact, suggests that people often need a crisis – a "disorienting dilemma"– that affects them personally – one way or another – to be shaken from their complacent convictions (Mezirow 1991). For some, becoming deathly ill with COVID-19 has in fact been such a transformative experience.

In some ways, climate change and COVID-19 offer an interesting test of this proposition. In the case of climate change, part of the problem is that for most people there is no immediate personal experience of a crisis, at least in the usual sense of crisis. The indicators of a coming crisis are all present, but the specific circumstances have not yet arrived to affect the everyday lives of most people. It is also relatively easy to propose measures to deal with climate change: renewable energy, more efficient transport systems, more energy-efficient buildings and the like – all things that can improve our way of life. On the other hand, COVID-19 is an immediate danger. It can be dangerous to simply leave the house. And the prescriptions are both uncomfortable and uncertain. Whereas in the case of climate crisis, we mainly find the learning to be slow and insufficient, in the matter of COVID-19 we do in fact find learning and action going on at both the societal and the personal/citizen level. Indeed, there is an intense international effort to learn more about the virus. The problem is that a small minority of deniers can cause a good deal of trouble for a majority.

A major factor contributing to this resistance to learning is the role of emotion. Serving as a barrier to organizing deliberative processes designed to deal with these post-truth issues, emotionally laden questions – *Gefühlsfragen* in German – wall off those who disagree from one another. As we saw, contemporary societies such as the United States and Britain are divided into political tribes hostile to each other. This dislike is embedded in the inner emotional landscapes that undergird these orientations. If one is predisposed to disliking those on the other side of an issue, everything they say will be clouded by these emotional landscapes. Painted in dark and foreboding colors, messages will be received with skepticism, distrust and even anger. In the face of cognitive dissonance between particular beliefs and given realities, emotional anxieties will work to patch over or block out the discrepancies. Policy professionals, in this case, will have to accept that the problem has left their sphere and moved into the realm of psychology. Policy knowledge remains an important part of the discussion, but it cannot break down the emotional barriers. Short of emotional reconciliation, though, the policy analyst needs to be aware of this subjective dynamic in organizing deliberative processes.

Emotional tensions thus pose a serious and sizable challenge to learning. City planners and others have developed interpretive-analytic methods for coming to grips with this problem (Fischer 2009: 285–292). These offer procedures to bring people together in structured ways that permit them to first express their emotional grievances to one tell them, without interruption, how they interpret their problematic situations. After letting out their emotions, the groups are allowed to question one another. Practitioners have found that after getting these emotionally charged statements out of the way, it is possible to more easily move to a deliberative process that emphasizes the need to learn the facts of the situation. There are, however, no guarantees.

This is a process that can only work in smaller group "mini-publics" (Fung 2006). It does not readily lend itself to a political situation involving a country as a whole. That is, while it is possible to deal with such problems in small groups, a nation divided into warring political tribes is yet another thing. It may take a genuine crisis to bring two warring camps together. But this will also depend on the effectiveness of a good deal of political work, and the quality of the leadership that undertakes it.

A precondition to such a deliberative possibility is stronger regulation of the social media. Until the ability of the disinformation industry to exploit the internet is curtailed, it will be exceedingly difficult to establish a common political ground for policy learning capable of grappling with the many problems that have piled up as a result of an extreme form of divisive government.

A second precondition involves our understanding of knowledge itself. Arriving at such an understanding necessitates a better grasp in the general public of the nature of knowledge and its production. This is a task for educators who have all too often assumed that their ways of thinking and their interpretations are superior to those of the lower and working classes (Sandel 2020). Not only do they need to update their understanding of what it means to talk about facts, especially in a social context, they also have to find ways to speak in the everyday language of ordinary citizens.

A third precondition is the presence of political leaders who are able and willing to talk across boundaries in an effort to move the society out of the impasse. This requires politicians who do not exploit gaps, misunderstandings and mutual suspicions for their own immediate political benefits. It requires leaders who are ready and capable of educating their citizens to interpretively understand the hard facts about the current situation and the need to come together, perhaps even in the name of survival. It's a political requirement that is as big as it is important.

With these points in mind, we nonetheless have to concede that nobody at this point knows how to bring these duplicitous practices of post-truth to a halt. It is customary for liberal commentators to point to the need for citizens to learn how to detect and interpret deceptive and false arguments, to plead for a better balance in media reporting on topics, to introduce new methods of civic political education in the schools focused on critical thinking, and, among other approaches, to innovate more effective communicative strategies on the part of scientific experts (Lewandowsky et al. 2017; D'Ancona 2017). While all of these measures require attention, they do not in and of themselves override the need for more rigorous public regulation of big tech media companies and greater attention and responsiveness to the economic, political and cultural realities of the forgotten segments of society. Reducing the economic and social insecurities of anxious citizens needs to be a crucial part of the effort to undercut post-truth politics.

To the degree possible, it is important to find ways to directly engage the denialists. It is essential to step into the political void and involve them in authentic deliberations about the interpretation of the "facts" and their social and political consequences. We need to develop meaningful public dialogue that takes us beyond acrimonious rhetoric to facilitate serious thinking about this dangerous situation. Having such a dialogue would depend on the possibility of breaking down the tribal barriers and building enough trust to enable people in the tribal camps to engage in reasoned deliberation. There are, to be sure, no assurances. In fact, at the present time, such an outcome appears to be unlikely.

The challenge ahead should not be underestimated. At stake here is the relation of science to public policy, the health of people around the world, the ecological fate of the planet and the future of democratic politics. The outcome of this struggle with post-truth politics will depend on the ability of the forces of reason to politically counter post-truth politics and its spread of deceptive information and outright lies. There is nothing easy about this project. Both climate change and COVID-19 denial are moving topics. Given the complicated issues associated with both issues, much of what is written about them today can sound outmoded tomorrow. Nonetheless, interpretive policy analysis, as policy Element will hopefully play a role, however minor, in the effort to better understand the interpretive dynamics of the argumentative struggle and the processes of policy politics of which it is an essential part.

References

Ahmed, S. (2014). *The Cultural Politics of Emotion*. Edinburgh: University of Edinburgh Press.

Allen, B. B. (2017). Second Only to Nuclear War: Science and the Making of Existential Threat in Global Climate Governance. *International Studies Quarterly*, 61 809–820.

Al Tamimi, K. (2016). Evaluating Narrative Arguments. https://core.ac.uk /download/pdf/84725259.pdf

Andersen, K. (2017). How American Lost its Mind. *The Atlantic*. December 18.

Anderson, C. A. (1978). The Logic of Public Problems: Evaluation in *Comparative Policy Research*. In D. E. Ashford, ed., *Comparing Public Policies: New Concepts and Methods*. Beverly Hills: Sage Publications, pp. 19–42.

Anderson, J. (2020). She Hunts Viral Rumors about Real Viruses. *New York Times*. October 13.

Arantani, L. (2020). They're Rooting for the Coronavirus: Trump Allies Attack Democrats and the Media. *The Guardian*. March 5. www.theguardian.com /world/2020/mar/05/theyre-rooting-for-the-coronavirus-trump-allies-attack-democrats-and-the-media

Archer, M., Bhaskar, R. Collier, A., Lawson, T. and Norrie, A. eds. (1998). *Critical Realism: Essential Readings*. London: Routledge.

Arendt, H. (1972). *Crisis of the Republic*. New York: Harcourt Brace Jovanovich.

Aristotle. (1991). *On Rhetoric: Theory of Civic Discourse*. Translated by G. A. Kennedy. Oxford: Oxford University Press.

Bächtiger, A., Dryzek, J. S., Mansbridge, J. and Warren, M. eds. (2018). *Oxford Handbook of Deliberative Democracy*. Oxford: Oxford University Press.

Baker, P. (2020). Dishonesty Has Defined Trump Presidency: The Consequences Could Be Lasting. *New York Times*. November 1. www .nytimes.com/2020/11/01/us/politics/trump-presidency-dishonesty.html? referringSource=articleShare

Ball, J. (2017). *Post-Truth: How Bullshit Conquered the World*. London/Hull: Biteback Publishing.

Ball, P. (2020). Anti-Vaccination Movement Could Undermine Efforts to End Coronavirus Pandemic, Experts Warn. *Nature*. May 13.

Bennett, L. and Livingston, S. (2018). The Disinformation Order: Disruptive Communication and the Decline of Democratic Institutions. *European Journal of Communication*, 33 (2): 122–139.

Bennett, L. W. and Livingston, S. eds. (2021). *The Disinformation Age. Politics, Technology, and Disruptive Communication in the United States*. Cambridge: Cambridge University Press.

Berger, P. (2006). Between Relativism and Fundamentalism. *The American Interest* 2(1).

Berger, P. and Luckmann T. (1965). *The Social Construction of Reality.* New York: Doubleday.

Berube, M. (2011). The Science Wars Redux, *Democracy Journal*, Winter (19): 64–74.

Best, J. (2012). *Damned Lies and Statistics: Untangling Numbers*. Berkeley: University of California Press.

Bokat-Lindell, S. 2021. Can the Unvaccinated be Persuaded? *New York Times.* August 3.

Boltanski, L. (2011). *On Critique: A Sociology of Emancipation*. Cambridge: Polity Press.

Bommel, S., Hulst, M., and Yanow, D. (2020). Interpretive Policy Analysis in the Netherlands. In F. van Nispen and P. Scholten, eds., *Policy Analysis and Evaluation in the Netherlands: Institutionalization and Performance*, pp 69–81.

Bourdieu, P. (1990). *The Logic of Practice*. Cambridge: Polity Press.

Cann, H. and Raymond, L. (2018). Does Climate Denialism Still Matter? The Prevalence of Alternative Frames in Opposition to Climate Policy. *Environmental Politics*, 27 (3): 1–22.

Chotiner, I. (2020). How to talk to Coronavirus Skeptics. *The New Yorker.* March 23.

Croucher, S. (2019). Trump Is a "Successful Sociopath" and a Predator Who "Lacks a Conscience and Lacks Empathy," Says Former Harvard Psychiatrist." *Newsweek*, October 29.

Czarniawska, B. (2021). The Production and the Reception of Fake News – Then and Now. Polonium Foundation, Webinar, January 13. www .youtube.com/watch?v=ppm4yij2N9k

D'Ancona, M. (2017). *Post Truth: The New War on Truth and How to Fight Back*. London: Ebury Press.

Davis, E. (2017). *Post-Truth: Why We Have Reached Peak Bullshit and What We Can Do About It*. London: Little Brown.

DeHaven-Smith, L. (1988). *Philosophical Critique of Policy Analysis: Lindblom, Habermas and the Great Society*. Gainsville: University of Florida Press.

Demelle, B. (2017). The Climate Denial Industry. www.beforetheflood.com /explore/thedeniers/the-climate-denial-industry/

Dewey, J. (1927). *The Public and Its Problems*. New York: Swallow.

Diesing, P. (1962). *Reason in Society: Five Types of Decisions in Their Social Context*. Urbana: University of Illinois Press.

Dunlap, R. E. and Jacques, P. J. (2013). Climate Change Denial Books and Conservative Think Tanks: Exploring the Connection. *American Behavioral Scientist*, 57 (6): 699–731.

Dunn, W. N. (2019). *Pragmatism and the Origins of the Policy Sciences: Rediscovering Lasswell and the Chicago School* (Elements in Public Policy). Cambridge: Cambridge University Press.

Durnova, A. (2019). *Understanding Emotions in Post-Factual Politics: Negotiating Truth*. Cheltenham: Edward Elgar Publishing.

Edelman, M. (1988). *Constructing the Public Spectacle*. Chicago: Chicago University Press.

Edwards, P. N. (2010). A *Vast Machine: Computer Models, Climate Data and the Politics of Global Warming*. Cambridge: MIT Press.

Eulau, H. ed. (1969). *Behavioralism in Political Science*. New York: Atherton.

Farkas J. and Schou, J. (2020). Post-Truth, Fake News and Democracy: Mapping the Politics. London: Routledge.

Fischer, F. (1995). *Evaluating Public Policy*. Belmont, CA: Wadsworth.

Fischer, F. (2000). *Citizens, Experts, and the Environment*. Durham, NC: Duke University Press.

Fischer, F. (2003). *Reframing Public Policy: Discursive Politics and Deliberative Practice*. Oxford: Oxford University Press.

Fischer, F. (2005). Are Scientists Irrational? Risk Assessment in Practical Reason. In M. Leach, I. Scoones and B. Wynne, eds. *Science and Citizens*. London: Zed: 54–65.

Fischer, F. (2007). Deliberative Policy Analysis as Practical Reason: Integrating Empirical and Normative Arguments, in F. Fischer, G. Miller, and M. Sidney, eds., Handbook of Public Policy Analysis. Theory, Politics and Methods. New York: Taylor and Francis, pp. 223–236.

Fischer, F. (2009). *Democracy and Expertise: Reorienting Policy Inquiry*. Oxford: Oxford University Press.

Fischer, F. (2017). *Climate Crisis and the Democratic Prospect: Participatory Governance in Sustainable Communities*. Oxford: Oxford University Press.

Fischer, F. (2019). Knowledge Politics and Post-Truth in Climate Denial: On the Social Construction of Alternative Facts. *Critical Policy Studies*, 3 (2): 33–152.

Fischer, F. (2020). Post-Truth Politics and Climate Denial: Further Reflections. *Critical Policy Studies*. 14 (1): 124–130.

Fischer F. and Boossabong, P. (2018). Deliberative Policy Analysis. In J. J. Dryzek, J. Mansbridge and M. Warren, eds. *Oxford Handbook of Deliberative Democracy*. Oxford: Oxford University Press, pp. 584–594.

Flood, A. (2016). "Post-Truth" Named Word of the Year by Oxford Dictionaries. *The Guardian.* November 15. www.theguardian.com/ books/2016/nov/15/post-truth-named-word-of-the-year-by-oxford-dictionaries

Forber, V. (2020). Covid Confusion. *Heartland Institute.* May 11. www .heartland.org/news-opinion/news/covid-confusion

Fortenbaugh, W. W. (1975). *Aristotle on Emotion.* London: Duckworth.

Foucault, M. (1991). *Discipline and Punishment: The Birth of the Prison.* New York: Random House.

Franks, S. (2014). The Scientific Method (and Other Heresies). In A. Moran, ed., *Climate Change: The Facts.* Melbourne: Institute of Public Affairs, pp. 252-263.

Franz, W. (1997). The Development of an Agenda for Climate Change: Connecting Science to Policy. *Interim Report.* International Institute for Applied Systems Analysis. IIASA, IR-97–034. Laxenburg, Austria.

Fuller, S. (2018). *Post Truth: Knowledge as a Power Game.* London: Anthem Press.

Fung, A. (2006). Varieties of Public Participation in Complex Governance. *Public Administration Review.* 66 (1): 66–75.

Gebrekidan, S. (2020). For Autocrats, and Others, Coronavirus Is a Chance to Grab Even More Power *New York Times.* March 31

Gibbins, J. R. and Reimer, B. (1999). *The Politics of Postmodernity.* London: Sage.

Gibbons, A. (2017). Postmodernism is Dead. What Comes Next? *Times Literary Supplement.* June 12. www.the-tls.co.uk/articles/postmodernism-dead-comes-next/

Gitlin, T. (2020). The Enigma of Constancy: The Resilience of Trump's Base. *Salmagundi*, No. 206–207, Spring–Summer: 67–94.

Graber, D. (2019). Against Economics. *New York Review of Books.* December 5. www.nybooks.com/articles/2019/12/05/against-economics/

Grauhan, R. and Strubelt, W. (1971). Political Rationality Reconsidered: Notes on an Integrated Scheme for Policy Choice. *Policy Sciences*, 2 (Summer): 270–281.

Grey, J. (2017). Post Truth by Matthew D'Ancona and Post-Truth by Evan Davis Review – Is This Really a New Era of Politics? *Guardian.* May 19. www.theguardian.com/books/2017/may/19/post-truth-matthew-dancona-evan-davis-reiews

Gubrium, J. F. and Holstein, J. A. (2009). *Analyzing Narrative Realities.* Newbury Park, CA: Sage Publications.

Haas, M. (1989). Do Regimes Matter? Epistemic Communities and Mediterranean Pollution. *International Organization*, 43 (3): 377–403.

Habermas, J. (1975). *Legitimation Crisis*. Cambridge: Polity Press.

Hajer, M. and Wagenaar, H. eds. (2003). *Deliberative Policy Analysis*. Cambridge: Cambridge University Press.

Harrison, C. (2004). Postmodern Principles for Responsive Reading Assessment. *Journal of Reading Research*. 27. 163–173. https://doi.org/10.1111/j.1467-9817.2004.00224.x.

Healey, P. (1997). *Collaborative Planning: Shaping Places in Fragmented Societies*. London: Palgrave.

Hofstadter, R. (2012). *The Paranoid Style in American Politics*. New York: Knopf Doubleday.

Hutcheon, L. (2003). *The Politics of Post-Modernism*. London: Routledge.

Jamieson, K. H. and Cappella, J. N. (2010). *Echo Chamber: Rush Limbaugh and the Conservative Media Establishment*. New York: Oxford University Press.

Jasanoff, S. (2004). *States of Knowledge: The Co-Production of Science and Social Order*. London: Routledge.

Jasanoff, S. and Simmet, H. R. (2017). No Funeral Bells: Public Reason in a "Post-Truth" Age. *Social Studies of Science*, 47 (5): 751–770.

John, T. (2020). Tens of Thousands of Britons have Died from Coronavirus, but Boris Johnson is Stoking a Cultural War. *CNN*, June 20. https://edition.cnn.com/2020/06/20/uk/boris-johnson-coronavirus-culture-wars-gbr-intl/index.html

Johnson, R. H. and Blair, J. A. (1996). Informal Logic and Critical Thinking. In F. van Eemeren, R. Grootendorst, and F. Snoeck Henkemans, eds. *Fundamentals of Argumentation Theory*. Mahwah, NJ: Lawrence Erlbaum Associates: 383–386.

Jones M. D., McBeth M. K. and Shanahan E. A. (2014). Introducing the Narrative Policy Framework. In M. D. Jones, E. A. Shanahan and M. K. McBeth, eds. *The Science of Stories*. New York: Palgrave Macmillan, pp. 1–25.

Kahan, D. M. (2010). Fixing the Communications Failure. *Nature*, 463: 296–297. https://doi.org/10.1038/463296a

Kahan, D. M. (2017). *The Cultural Cognition Project*. Yale Law School. http://www.culturalcognition.net/kahan/

Kakutani, M. (2018). *The Death of Truth: Notes on Falsehood in the Age of Trump*. New York: Tim Duggan Books.

Kavanagh, H. and Rich, M. (2020). *Truth Decay: An Initial Exploration of the Diminishing Role of Facts and Analysis in American Public Life*. Santa Monica, CA: Rand Corporation.

Keen, S. (2015). Narrative Emotions. In *Narrative Form*. Heidelberg: Springer, pp. 152–161.

Kessler, G., Rizzo, S. and Kelly, M. (2020). President Trump has Made More Than 20,000 False or Misleading Claims. *The Washington Post*. July 13. www.washingtonpost.com/politics/2020/07/13/president-trump-has-made-more-than-20000-false-or-misleading-claims/

Klein, J. A. (2005). *Global Deception: The UN's Stealth Assault on America's Freedoms*. Los Angeles: World Ahead Publishing.

Klein, N. (2011). Capitalism vs. the Climate. *The Nation*, November 9.

Kleres, J. (2010). Emotions and Narrative Analysis: Methodological Approach. *Journal for the Theory of Social Behavior*, 42 (2): 182–202.

Kolbert, E. (2017). That's What You Think: Why Reason and Evidence Won't Change our Minds. *The New Yorker*, February 27.

Krugman, P. (2020). World War C. The Covid-19 Story, Told in Lies. *New York Times*, June 30.

Kuhn, T. (1962). *The Structure of Scientific Revolutions*. Chicago: University of Chicago Press.

Laitman, M. (2020). Coronavirus and the Virus Hatred Against Jews. The Times of Israel. February 13. https://blogs.timesofisrael.com/coronavirus-and-the-virus-of-hatred-against-jews/.

Lasswell, H. (1971). *Pre-View of Policy Science*. New York: American Elsevier Publishing.

Lasswell, H. and Kaplan, A. (1950). *Power and Society: A Framework of Political Inquiry*. New Haven, CT: Yale University Press.

Lasswell, H. and Lerner, D. eds. (1951). *The Policy Sciences*. Stanford: Stanford University Press.

Latour, B. (2017). Why Has Critique Run out of Steam? From Matters of Fact to Matters of Concern. *Critical Inquiry*, 30 (2): 2004.

Latour, B. (2018). *Down to Earth: Politics in the New Climatic Regime*. Cambridge: Cambridge, UK Polity Press.

Latour, B. and Woolgar, S. (1986). *Laboratory Life: The Social Construction of Scientific Facts*. Princeton: Princeton University Press.

Lewandowsky, S., Ecker, U. and Cook, J. (2017). Beyond Misinformation: Understanding and Coping with the "Post-Truth" Era. *Journal of Applied Research in Memory and Cognition*, 6 (4): 353–369.

Lewis, M. (2016). American Political Parties are Just Tribes Now. *The Daily Beast*. January 2. www.thedailybeast.com/americas-political-parties-are-just-tribes-now.

Lindblom, C. and Cohen, D. K. (1979). *Usable Knowledge: Social Science and Social Problem Solving*. New Haven, CT: Yale University Press.

Lomborg, B. (2001). *The Skeptical Environmentalist*. Cambridge: Cambridge University Press.

Lundberg, H. (2013). Karl Mannheim's Sociology of Political Knowledge. *E-International Relations*. https://www.e-ir.info/pdf/43807

MacIntyre, A. (2007). *After Virtue*. 3rd ed. South Bend: University of Notre Dame Press.

Mackintosh, E. (2020). No Matter Who Wins the US Election, the World's "Fake News" Problem is Here to Stay. *CNN*, October 25. https://edition .cnn.com/2020/10/25/world/trump-fake-news-legacy-intl/index.html

MacRae, D. (1976). *The Social Function of Social Science*. New Haven, CT: Yale University Press.

Mannheim, K. (1936). *Ideology and Utopia*. New York: Harcourt, Brace and World.

Mannheim, K. (1986 [1925]). *Conservatism*. London and New York: Routledge & Kegan Paul.

Markus, G. E. (2002). *The Sentimental Citizen: Emotion in Democratic Politics*. University Park, PA: Penn State University Press.

Martelle, S. (2020). "LIBERATE MICHIGAN!" Trump Tweets to Armed Protesters. What Was He Thinking? *Los Angeles Times*. April 17. www .latimes.com/opinion/story/2020-04-17/liberate-michigan-trump-tweets -2nd-amendment-coronavirus-pandemic

McDermott, R. (2019). Psychological Underpinnings of Post-Truth in Policy Beliefs. *PS: Political Science and Politics*. April: 218–222.

McInytre, L. (2018). *Post-Truth*. Cambridge: MIT Press.

Mezirow, J. (1991). *Transformative Dimensions of Adult Learning*. San Francisco, CA: Jossey-Bass.

Miller, C. (2004). Climate Science and the Making of a Global Political Order, in S. Jasanoff, ed., *States of Knowledge: The Co-Production of Science and the Social Order*. New York: Routledge, pp. 46–66.

Miller, H. (2020). *Narrative Politics in Public Policy: Legalizing Cannibis*. New York: Springer.

Moyer, M. W. (2019). People Drawn to Conspiracy Theories Share a Cluster of Psychological Features. *The Scientific American*, March 1. https://www .scientificamerican.com/article/people-drawn-to-conspiracy-theories-share -a-cluster-of-psychological-features/

Münch, S. (2016). *Interpretative Policy-Analyse*. Wiesbaden: Springer.

Nichols, T. (2019). In Trump's World, Reality is Negotiable. *The Atlantic*, January 13. www.theatlantic.com/politics/archive/2019/01/donald-trump- rejects-expertise/579808/

Nolte, J. (2020). All the Establishment Media's Dangerous Coronavirus Lies. *Breitbart*, March 17. www.breitbart.com/the-media/2020/03/17/nolte-all-the -establishment-medias-dangerous-coronavirus-lies/

Nurius, P. (2013). *Cognition and Social Cognitive Theory Encyclopedia of Social Work*. Published online: 11 June 2013. https://doi.org/10.1093/acre fore/9780199975839.013.65

Nussbaum, M. (2001). *Upheavals of Thought: The Intelligence of Emotions*. Cambridge: Cambridge University Press.

Nyhan, B. (2021). Why the Backfire Effect Does Not Explain the Durability of Political Misperceptions. *Proceeding of the National Academy of Sciences*, 118 (15): e1912440117.

Ornstein, N. and Mann, T. E. (2016). *It's Even Worse Than It Looks: How the American Constitutional System Collided with the New Politics of Extremism*. New York: Basic Books.

Orwell, S. and Angus, I. eds. (1980). *The Collected Essays, Journalism and Letters of George Orwell*, Vol. II. New York: Harcourt, Brace and World.

Packer, G. (2018). A New Report Offers Insights Into Tribalism in the Age of Trump. *New Yorker*, October 13. www.newyorker.com/news/daily-comment /a-new-report-offers-insights-into-tribalism-in-the-age-of-trump

Pappas, P. (2011). Climate Scientist Calls Hacked "Climategate" Emails "Truly Pathetic." *Live Science*, November 22.

Perl, A., Howlett, M. and Ramesh, M. (2018). Policy-Making and Truthiness: Can Existing Policy Models Cope With Politicized Evidence and Willful Ignorance in a "Post-Fact" World? *Policy Sciences*, 51(4): 581–600.

Pinker, S. (2018). The Intellectual War on Science: It's Wreaking Havoc in Universities and Jeopardizing the Progress of Research. *The Chronicle of Higher Education*, February 13.

Plough, A. and Krimsky, S. (1987). The Emergence of Risk Communication Studies: Social and Political Context. *Science, Technology and Human Values*, 12 (3–4): 4–10.

Pogrebinschi, T. and Samuels, D. (2014). The Impact of Participatory Democracy: Evidence from Brazil's National Public Policy Conferences. *Comparative Politics*, 46 (3): 313–332.

Porter T. (1995). *Trust in Numbers: The Pursuit of Objectivity in Science and Public Life*. Princeton: Princeton University Press.

Proctor, R. (2008). Agnatology: A Missing Term to Describe the Cultural Production of Ignorance (and Its Study). In R. Proctor and L. Schiebinger, eds. *The Making and Unmasking of Ignorance*. Stanford: Stanford University Press, pp. 1–36.

Proctor, R. and Schiebinger, L. eds. (2008). *The Making and Unmaking of Ignorance*. Stanford: Stanford University Press.

Rabinow, P. and Sullivan, W. M. eds. (1987). *Interpretive Social Science: A Reader*. Berkeley: University of California Press.

Rauch, J. (2021). *The Constitution of Knowledge: A Defense of Truth.* Washington, DC: The Brookings Institution.

Rawls, J. A. (1971). *A Theory of Justice.* Cambridge: Harvard University Press.

Robert, C. and Zechhauser, R. (2010). The Methodology of Positive Policy Analysis. *Working Paper Series* RWP10-041, John F. Kennedy School of Government, Harvard University https://ideas.repec.org/p/ecl/harjfk/rwp10-041.html

Roe, E. (1994). *Narrative Policy Analysis.* Durham, NC: Duke University Press.

Roe, E. (2020). When Complex is as Simple as it Gets. https://mess-and-reliability.blog/. Published October 22, 2020.

Rosenau, P. M. (1992). *Postmodernism and the Social Sciences.* Princeton: Princeton University Press.

Rosenblum, N. L. and Muirhead, R. (2019). *A Lot of People Are Saying: The New Conspiracism and the Assault on Democracy.* Princeton: Princeton University Press.

Ross, W. (1996). *Science Wars.* Durham, NC: Duke University Press.

Sabatier, P. A., (1988). An Advocacy Coalition Framework of Policy Change and the Role of Policy-Oriented Learning Therein. *Policy Sciences*, 21(June): 129–168.

Sandel, M. J. (2020). Disdain for the Less Educated Is the Last Acceptable Prejudice. *New York Times*, September 2. www.nytimes.com/2020/09/02/opinion/education-prejudice.html?referringSource=articleShare

Sandman, P. (1987). Risk Communication: Facing Public Outrage. *US EPA Journal*, November: 21–22.

Schield, M. (2007). "Teaching the Social Construction of Statistics," *Research Gate*. www.researchgate.net/publication/277299441_Teaching_the_Social_Construction_of_Statistics.

Schmid. A. (1989). *Cost-Benefit Analysis: A Political Economy Approach.* Boulder, CO: Westview Press.

Schneider, A. L. and Ingram, H. eds. (2006). *Deserving and Entitled: Social Constructions and Public Policy.* Albany, NY: SUNY Press.

Schneider, A. and Ingram, H. (2013). *Social Construction of Target Populations: Implications for Politics and Policy.* Cambridge University Press (online: September 2, 2013).

Schoenfeld, A., Walker, L. A. S., Jones, L. W. and Gamio, L. (2020). Is the Corona Death Tally Inflated: Here is why the Experts Say No. *New York Times*, June 20.

Schuman, D. (1982). *Policy Analysis, Education, and Everyday Life.* Toronto: D. C. Heath.

Scriven, M. (1987). Probative Logic. In F. H. Van Eemeren, R. Grootendorst, J. A. Blair and C. A. Willard. eds. *Argumentation: Across the Lines of Discipline*. Amsterdam: Foris.

Sen, A. (1993). Capability and Well-Being. In M. C. Nussbaum and A. Sen, eds. *The Quality of Life*. Oxford: Oxford University Press, pp. 30–53.

Shear, M., Haberman, M. and Herdon, S. (2020). Trump Rally Fizzles as Attendance Falls Short of Campaign's Expectations. *New York Times*, June 21. www.boston.com/news/politics/2020/06/21/trump-rally-fizzles-as-crowd-size-falls-short-of-campaigns-expectations

Slessor, C. (2020). Why Do Coronavirus Sceptics and Deniers Continue to Downplay the Disease. *ABC News*, May 2. www.abc.net.au/news/2020-05-03/coronavirus-sceptics-continue-to-downplay-covid19/12201344

Slovic, P., Fischhoff, B. and Lichtenstein, S. (1979). Rating the Risks. *Environment*, 21: 36–39.

Sokal, A. D. (2008). *Beyond the Hoax: Science, Philosophy and Culture*. Oxford: Oxford University Press.

Stanford Encyclopedia of Philosophy. (2020). Relativism. Stanford: Stanford University Press.

Stephens. B. (2020). Biden's Loose Lips Could Sink His Chance. *New York Times*, August 24: 23.

Stillitoe, P. (2007). Local Science vs Global Science: An Overview. In Stillitoe, P. ed. *Local Science vs Global Science*. Oxford: Berghahn, pp. 1–22.

Stone, D. (1988). *Policy Paradox and Political Reason*. Glenview, IL; Scott Foresman.

Stone, D. (2020). *Counting: How We Use Numbers to Decide What Matters*. New York: W. W. Norton.

Sullivan, R. (2020). Coronavirus: FDA Chief Disputes Trump's Claim "Deep State" is Delaying Vaccine Until After US Election. *Independent*, August 25. www.independent.co.uk/news/world/americas/us-politics/coronavirus-fda-chief-trump-claim-vaccine-delay-us-election-deep-state-a9687271.html

Taylor, P. (1961). *Normative Discourse*. Englewood Cliffs, NJ: Prentice-Hall.

Thies, C. (2020). The Real Threat of Viruses. *Heartland Institute*. February 10. www.heartland.org/news-opinion/news/the-real-threat-of-viruses

Tormey, S. (2016). The Contemporary Crisis of Representative Democracy. *Parliament of Australia, Papers on Parliament*, No. 66. www.aph.gov.au/About_Parliament/Senate/Powers_practice_n_procedures/pops/Papers_on_Parliament_66/The_Contemporary_Crisis_of_Representative_Democracy

Toulmin, S. (1958). *The Uses of Argument*. Cambridge: Cambridge University Press.

van Bommel, S.. Hulst, M. Yanow, D. 2020. Interpretive Policy Analysis in the Netherlands, in van Nispen and P. Scholten eds. *Policy Analysis and Evaluation in the Netherlands: Institutionalization and Performance.* Bristol: Policy Press

Vence, T. and Grant, B. (2017). March for Science: Dispatches from Washington, D.C. *The Scientist*, April 21. www.the-scientist.com/daily-news/march-for-science-dispatches-from-washington-dc–31632

Vosoughi, S., Roy, D. and Aral, S. (2018). The Spread of True and False News Online. *Science*, 359 (6380), March 9, 2018: 1146–1151.

Warzel, C. (2019). Why Trump Tweeted About Civil War. *New York Times*, September 30. www.nytimes.com/2019/09/30/opinion/trump-civil-war.html

Warzel, C. (2020). Is QAnon the Most Dangerous Conspiracy Theory of the 21st Century. *New York Times*, April 4.

Watson, B. (2016). *Stephen Colbert: Beyond Truthiness*. Cleveland, OH: New Word City. www.nytimes.com/2020/08/04/opinion/qanon-conspiracy-theory -arg.html?referringSource=articleShare

Waugh, R. (2011). New Leak of Hacked Global Warming Scientist Emails: A "Smoking Gun" Proving a Conspiracy – Or Just Hot Air? *Mail Online*, November 22. www.dailymail.co.uk/sciencetech/article-2064826/New-leak-hacked-global-warming-scientist-emails-A-smoking-gun-proving-conspir acy–just-hot-air.html

Weimer, D. L. and Vining, A. R. (2017). *Policy Analysis: Concepts and Practice*. New York: Routledge.

Wilson, J. (2020). The Rightwing Christian Preachers in Deep Denial Over Covid-19's Danger. *The Guardian*, April 4.

Yanow, D. (2000). *Conducting Interpretive Policy Analysis*. Thousand Oaks, CA: Sage Publications.

Yanow, D. and Schwartz-Shea, P. (2006). *Interpretations and Method: Empirical Research and the Interpretive Turn*. Armonk, NY: M. F. Sharpe.

Young, K., Ashby, D. Boaz, A. and Grayson, L. (2002). Social Science and the Evidence-Based Policy Movement. *Social Policy and Society*, 1 (3): 215–224.

Zimmer, B. (2010). Truthiness. *New York Times*, October 13. https://www .nytimes.com/2010/10/17/magazine/17FOB-onlanguage-t.html

Acknowledgments

I wish to acknowledge a number of people for their helpful comments along the way. It is difficult to list all of the people who, in various ways, have had an influence on this work. But I can more easily thank those who directly assisted by reading and discussing parts of the manuscript. Thanks go in particular to Alan Mandell, Douglas Torgerson, Ingofur Blühdorn, Hugh Miller, Susan Fainstein, Piyapong Boossabong, Edgar Göll, Rosanna Boullosa, Philippe Zittoun, Dorota Stasiak, Lance Bennett, Melina Proestou, Danniel Gobbi, Michael Haus, Rosana Boullosa, Navdeep Mathur, Kathrin Braun, M. Ramesh, Richard Rosen, Hubertus Buchstein and, not least, Sabine Braun-Fischer.

Frank Fischer is Distinguished Professor Emeritus of Politics and Global Affairs at Rutgers University, a Faculty Fellow in Politics at the University of Kassel and a Research Associate at Humboldt University in Germany. He has written numerous books and essays and has received Harold Lasswell and Aaron Wildavsky Awards for contributions to the field of public policy.

Public Policy

M. Ramesh

National University of Singapore (NUS)

M. Ramesh is UNESCO Chair on Social Policy Design at the Lee Kuan Yew School of Public Policy, NUS. His research focuses on governance and social policy in East and Southeast Asia, in addition to public policy institutions and processes. He has published extensively in reputed international journals. He is Co-editor of *Policy and Society* and *Policy Design and Practice*.

Michael Howlett

Simon Fraser University, British Colombia

Michael Howlett is Burnaby Mountain Professor and Canada Research Chair (Tier 1) in the Department of Political Science, Simon Fraser University. He specialises in public policy analysis, and resource and environmental policy. He is currently editor-in-chief of *Policy Sciences* and co-editor of the *Journal of Comparative Policy Analysis, Policy and Society* and *Policy Design and Practice*.

Xun WU

Hong Kong University of Science and Technology

Xun WU is Professor and Head of the Division of Public Policy at the Hong Kong University of Science and Technology. He is a policy scientist whose research interests include policy innovations, water resource management and health policy reform. He has been involved extensively in consultancy and executive education, his work involving consultations for the World Bank and UNEP.

Judith Clifton

University of Cantabria

Judith Clifton is Professor of Economics at the University of Cantabria, Spain. She has published in leading policy journals and is editor-in-chief of the *Journal of Economic Policy Reform*. Most recently, her research enquires how emerging technologies can transform public administration, a forward-looking cutting-edge project which received €3.5 million funding from the Horizon2020 programme.

Eduardo Araral

National University of Singapore (NUS)

Eduardo Araral is widely published in various journals and books and has presented in forty conferences. He is currently Co-Director of the Institute of Water Policy at the Lee Kuan Yew School of Public Policy, NUS, and is a member of the editorial board of *Journal of Public Administration Research and Theory* and the board of the Public Management Research Association.

About the series

Elements in Public Policy is a concise and authoritative collection of assessments of the state of the art and future research directions in public policy research, as well as substantive new research on key topics. Edited by leading scholars in the field, the series is an ideal medium for reflecting on and advancing the understanding of critical issues in the public sphere. Collectively, it provides a forum for broad and diverse coverage of all major topics in the field while integrating different disciplinary and methodological approaches.

Cambridge Elements ≡

Public Policy

Elements in the series

A full series listing is available at: www.cambridge.org/EPPO